CONTEMPLATING
CHRIST WITH LUKE

Cardinal George Pell

Published in 2012 by Connor Court Publishing Pty Ltd

Copyright © Cardinal George Pell 2012

ALL RIGHTS RESERVED. This book contains material protected under International and Federal Copyright Laws and Treaties. Any unauthorised reprint or use of this material is prohibited. No part of this book may be reproduced or transmitted in any form or by any means, electronic or mechanical, including photocopying, recording, or by any information storage and retrieval system without express written permission from the publisher.

Connor Court Publishing Pty Ltd.
PO Box 1
Ballan VIC 3342
sales@connorcourt.com
www.connorcourt.com

ISBN: 9781922168054 (pbk.)

Cover design by Ian James

Printed in Australia

Painting by Francisco (Kiko) Argüello, cofounder of the Neo-Catechumenal Way, and is to be found in the Church of the Most Holy Trinity, Piacenza, Italy. It is used with his permission.

CONTENTS

1. INTRODUCTION 1
2. 1ST SUNDAY OF ADVENT. Luke 21:25-8; 34-36
   The Lord will come again 7
3. 2ND SUNDAY OF ADVENT. Luke 3:1-6
   A Baptism of Repentance for the Forgiveness of Sins 12
4. 3RD SUNDAY OF ADVENT. Luke 3:10-18
   "What must we do?" 17
5. 4TH SUNDAY OF ADVENT. Luke 1:39-44
   Blessed is the Fruit of Your Womb 21
6. CHRISTMAS MIDNIGHT MASS (i). Luke 2:1-14
   The First Crib 25
7. CHRISTMAS MIDNIGHT MASS (ii). Luke 2:1-14
   Christmas Gifts 28
8. NEW YEAR'S DAY. Luke 2:16-21
   Not an Eternal Cycle of Return 30
9. THE HOLY FAMILY. Luke 2:41-52
   Many Problems 33
10. 1ST SUNDAY IN ORDINARY TIME. Luke 3:15-6.21-2
    Baptism of the Lord 37
11. 3RD & 4TH SUNDAYS IN ORDINARY TIME. Luke 1:1-4, 4:14-30
    The Spirit of the Lord is Upon Me 41
12. 5TH SUNDAY IN ORDINARY TIME. Luke 5:1-11
    Called 45
13. 6TH SUNDAY IN ORDINARY TIME. Luke 6:17, 20-26
    Blessings and Curses 49

14.	7TH SUNDAY IN ORDINARY TIME. Luke 6:27-38	
	Love Your Enemies..	52
15.	8TH SUNDAY IN ORDINARY TIME. Luke 6:39-45	
	The Blind should not lead the Blind...	56
16.	1ST SUNDAY OF LENT. Luke 4:1-13	
	Christ Tempted Also...	59
17.	2ND SUNDAY OF LENT. Luke 9:28-36	
	Why Transfigured?..	63
18.	3RD SUNDAY OF LENT. Luke 13:1-9	
	St. Patrick and Enduring Faith..	67
19.	4TH SUNDAY OF LENT. Luke 15:1-3:11-32	
	Our Loving Father and his Older Son......................................	72
20.	PALM SUNDAY (i). Luke 19:28-40	
	The Entry into Jerusalem..	76
21.	PALM SUNDAY (ii). Luke 22:14-23:56	
	The Start of Holy Week..	79
22.	CHRISM MASS OF HOLY WEEK. Luke 4:16-21	
	Anointed..	81
23.	EASTER NIGHT MASS. Luke 24:1-12	
	Empty Tomb..	85
24.	3RD SUNDAY OF EASTER – (YEAR A). Luke 24:13-35	
	New Sight at Emmaus...	89
25.	3RD SUNDAY OF EASTER – (YEAR B). Luke 24:35-48	
	Physical Resurrection?..	92
26.	7TH SUNDAY OF EASTER – ASCENSION DAY. Luke 24:46-53	
	Priests and Leaders Needed..	96
27.	PENTECOST SUNDAY. Acts 2:1-11	
	New Courage..	99

28.	FEAST OF CORPUS CHRISTI. Luke 9:11-17	
	The Body and Blood of Christ...	105
29.	9TH SUNDAY IN ORDINARY TIME. Luke: 7:1-10	
	Unworthy but Faithful..	109
30.	10TH SUNDAY IN ORDINARY TIME. Luke 7.11-16	
	Resurrection...	113
31.	11TH SUNDAY IN ORDINARY TIME. Luke 7:36-8:3	
	Forgiveness...	116
32.	12TH SUNDAY IN ORDINARY TIME. Luke 9:18-24	
	The Divine Redeemer...	120
33.	13TH SUNDAY IN ORDINARY TIME. Luke 9:51-62	
	No Fire and Brimstones...	124
34.	14TH SUNDAY IN ORDINARY TIME. Luke 10:1-12.17-20	
	Written in the Book of Life..	128
35.	15TH SUNDAY IN ORDINARY TIME. Luke 10:25-37	
	Jesus and the Good Samaritan (i)...	131
36.	15TH SUNDAY IN ORDINARY TIME. Luke 10:25-37	
	A Second approach to the Good Samaritan (ii)...................................	136
37.	16TH SUNDAY IN ORDINARY TIME. Luke 10:38-42	
	Mary and Martha...	139
38.	17TH SUNDAY IN ORDINARY TIME. Luke 11:1-13	
	Jesus' Prayer...	143
39.	18TH SUNDAY IN ORDINARY TIME. Luke 12:13-21	
	Poverty or Possessions?...	147
40.	19TH SUNDAY IN ORDINARY TIME. Luke 12:32-48	
	Ready for Action...	150
41.	20TH SUNDAY IN ORDINARY TIME. Luke 12:49-52	
	Fire and Division..	153

42.	21ST SUNDAY IN ORDINARY TIME. Luke 13:22-30 The Good Thief..	157
43.	22ND SUNDAY IN ORDINARY TIME. Luke 14:1, 7-14 Move Up Higher...	162
44.	23RD SUNDAY IN ORDINARY TIME. Luke 14:25-33 Who Comes First?...	166
45.	24TH SUNDAY IN ORDINARY TIME. Luke 15:1-32 The Parable of the Prodigal Son..	170
46.	25TH SUNDAY IN ORDINARY TIME. Luke 16:1-13 The Wisdom of the Sinner..	171
47.	26TH SUNDAY IN ORDINARY TIME. Luke 16:19-31 Who Will be First in Heaven?...	175
48.	27TH SUNDAY IN ORDINARY TIME. Luke 17:5-10 The Duties of Servants..	179
49.	28TH SUNDAY IN ORDINARY TIME. Luke 17:11-19 One Grateful Leper...	183
50.	29TH SUNDAY IN ORDINARY TIME. Luke 18:1-8 No Faith?...	187
51.	30TH SUNDAY IN ORDINARY TIME. Luke 18:9-14 The Pharisee Condemned...	189
52.	31ST SUNDAY IN ORDINARY TIME. Luke 19:1-10 The Rich Convert..	192
53.	32ND SUNDAY IN ORDINARY TIME. Luke 20:27-38 God of the Living..	196
54.	33RD SUNDAY IN ORDINARY TIME. Luke 21:5-19 Terrible Times...	200
55.	34TH SUNDAY – FEAST OF CHRIST THE KING. Luke 23:35-43 The King of the Jews..	204
56.	THE ASSUMPTION OF OUR LADY. Luke 1:39-56 Body and Soul...	210

INTRODUCTION

When I was putting together my thoughts on the Sunday readings from Luke's gospel a close friend remarked spontaneously, "Luke's is a beautiful gospel".

Generally our translations of the gospels are written in better English than the original Greek, especially of Matthew and Mark, even though we do not have one commonly accepted favourite New Testament translation, unlike the single new translation of the Roman Missal, to replace the much admired King James Version of the Anglicans, published in 1611 and enormously influential in the development of the English language. It was written to be proclaimed, a surprising masterpiece given that there were fifty four translators, Anglicans and Puritans, bishops and scholars.

All the New Testament is written in Greek, not Latin as some of us wrongly supposed and Luke's Greek is the best according to the experts.

As a Gentile, not Jewish, and probably one of the first Christian converts in Antioch, Greek would have been Luke's first or second language. Greek was then the common language around the Eastern Mediterranean areas, somewhat as English is today in many parts of the world and Luke wrote it stylishly.

This gospel has been popular across the centuries and in every continent and has not been "captured" by any one denomination. One could say its appeal is ecumenical.

St. Jerome, who translated the Bible into Latin late in the fourth century, described Luke as "a physician from Antioch, a man familiar with the Greek language, as can be seen from his writings, a follower of the apostle Paul and his companion on his journeys".

Our principal source of history for the early Church is the Acts of the Apostles, also written by Luke and the words of both these works, following St. Jerome once again, "act as medicine for the ailing soul". The historian Eusebius, also from the fourth century, wrote along the same lines, that they were "two medical books" to heal not our bodies, but our souls.

In his elegant prologue, which parallels the conventional introductions to Greek histories, Luke explains that he has gathered evidence from the early eyewitnesses and ministers of the word, and organised this material in an orderly fashion, so that his readers and especially his patron Theophilus (the God lover), "may know the truth concerning the things of which you have been informed (1:4)".

One strange characteristic of Jesus is that he left us no writings of his own, while the only evidence that he might have been able to write is in chapter eight of John's gospel where he drew some unknown figures or letters in the dust to save the adulterous woman from a death by stoning.

Our stricter Protestant friends, especially the Evangelicals with their appeal to "Sola Scriptura", scripture alone, and their aversion to normative tradition have a considerable problem from the fact that the first New Testament writings only began with Paul's first epistle to the Thessalonians around 51-2 A.D., nearly twenty years after Jesus' death.

The gospels were certainly later again and the traditional order of composition is Matthew, Mark, Luke and John, although many argue that Mark's gospel was written first. From Luke's introduction we know that he drew from the works and writings of others, probably St. Paul in particular.

Much time, energy and ink have been spent and spilt over the dates for the composition of each of the gospels. As is frequently the case in the New Testament we have a shortage of clear evidence, which has left much room for ingenuity, with estimates for the three synoptic gospels ranging over most of the second half of the first century A.D. The most common guesstimate for Luke is around 80 A.D.

All mainline Christians believe that the four canonical or approved gospels, i.e., "good news", were written under the inspiration of the Holy Spirit, by writers from within the Christian communities drawing from the earlier traditions. One can say accurately that the Church produced the gospels and then only "canonised" them as being the four approved accounts, and the only four such accounts in the second half of the second century, e.g., with St. Irenaeus, bishop of Lyons in Gaul (modern France). As a logical progression we need to have faith in the church as preserving the truth before we can have faith in the gospels and then progress to faith in Christ, the Son of God presented in the gospels. As the great North African theologian and bishop St. Augustine, who died in 430 A.D. wrote "I should not believe the gospel unless the authority of the Catholic Church moved me to do so" (*Against the Fundamental Epistle of Manichaeus*, c6). In other words we have the highest guarantees for Luke's gospel.

I had never realised, or perhaps I had forgotten, how much of our favourite information about Our Lord's sayings and doings is found only in Luke, although I was vividly aware of our dependency on him for the infancy narratives describing Our Lord's birth and its dramatic aftermaths.

Seven of Our Lord's parables are found only in his gospel, including the two favourites of the Good Samaritan and the Pharisee and the Tax collector in the temple. Without Luke we would not have the three great prayers or canticles, the *Benedictus, Magnificat* and *Nunc Dimittis*. We would not know of Zacchaeus climbing the sycamore tree, of Jesus weeping as he approached Jerusalem, of the Emmaus story, of the promise of salvation to the good thief. We hear more about the women of the New Testament in Luke.

Dante Alighieri (died 1321), the greatest Italian writer, the Italian Shakespeare, described Luke as the *"scriba mansuetudinis Christi"*, the writer who best captured the gentleness of Christ. This is true. In every sense Christ is at the centre of his gospel, even when he is emphasising the role of the Holy Spirit, but the strength and paradox of Christ's character is not hidden or underplayed.

We hear of Jesus' ugly confrontations with the Pharisees and scribes, of their unsuccessful efforts to trick him, of his regular provocation of the demons, their furious reactions, of his predictions that he must suffer, the grim progression to Calvary followed by the resurrection. Luke does not baulk at recounting the violence in Our Lord's parables, the severe beating for the unfaithful servant (12:47-8), the slaying of those who reject the king (19:27).

He also explicitly reports the terrible denunciations of the Pharisees and the lawyers, as fools and graves, guilty of the blood of the prophets shed from the foundation of the world (11:37-54). Public opinion today is often tempted to reduce Jesus to a milk and water figure, but Luke as a faithful and gifted storyteller presents him in all his bewildering splendour. Jesus is alternately kind and compassionate, passionately opposed to injustice and hypocrisy, ruthless with his opponents when they deserve it, kind and forgiving to the weak and repentant. After all Luke does have Jesus promising heaven "that very day" to the good thief.

By a strange twist the symbol for Luke's gospel is a calf, which St. Augustine connects with his emphasis on the priestly character of Our Lord where the calf was the typical victim sacrificed by the priest.

Legend also describes Luke as a portrait painter responsible for the beautiful icon of Our Lady and the Child Jesus in the basilica of Saint Mary Major in Rome known as *"Salus Populi Romani"*, the Salvation of the Roman people, after it was invoked during a plague in the time of Pope Gregory the Great. We used this image for the 2008 Sydney World Youth Day. The icon of Our Lady of Perpetual Help, which was once very popular in Australia and whose original from the eleventh or twelfth century is now found in the Redemptorist Church of St. Alphonsus, down the Via Merulana from St. Mary Major's, is also attributed to St. Luke. Both these figures of Our Lady are dressed like women from the later Christian empire of Byzantium, whose capital was Constantinople, now Istanbul and clearly are not Luke's work.

It is probably because the portrait of Jesus in his gospel is so sensitive and complete, with Jesus' compassion surmounting the occasional unexpected violence, that Luke came to be seen as a painter, especially of the young Jesus and his mother, which he describes so eloquently in his first two chapters.

Luke is a polished story teller, more eloquent than the other gospel writers, even if he is less dramatic than St. John at his best. We must be grateful, as St. Ambrose, the Archbishop of Milan in the second half of the fourth century pointed out because St. Luke "told us more about Our Lord's wonderful works than the other Evangelists".

"The Lord will come again"

1ST SUNDAY OF ADVENT
Jeremiah 33:14-16; Thessalonians 3:12-4:2;
Gospel: Luke 21:25-28; 34-36.

Many of us are often surprised to find that it is the First Sunday of Advent already; the beginning of the official period of preparation for the feast of Christmas. We know that the word "advent" derives from the Latin word "advenire" to come.

Similarly, most of us who are getting old are surprised and can hardly believe that so many years have passed. When we are very young we spend years waiting and hoping to be older; in our twenties and thirties we are unconcerned about these things if we are healthy. Then glimmers of wisdom develop, intimations of mortality, a little health scare here or there; and an awareness that time is running out, that we do not have forever to do what we desire.

For all these reasons, I thought a few words about the second meaning of Advent, about the Second Coming of the Lord at the end of time might be useful, i.e., about the Last Judgement, preceded by some reflections on what Christians mean by history.

Night follows day. The four seasons come around all too quickly. The Eastern religions speak of the everlasting wheel of return, the cyclical nature of reality, like the earth revolving around the sun. Today some scientists and philosophers deny that there is any point to all this repetition in nature. Human life is a gigantic meaningless fluke, a bleak view indeed.

The coming of the Son of God into history in a stable at Bethlehem is a marker event. It signals that something new and definitive has happened; God is with us. The world has changed by his birth and will change further with his death and resurrection and the redemption this will achieve.

We now take it for granted that history is moving forward, not always for the better, but is moving forward, not travelling in meaningless circles. The popular desire to believe in progress is strong, even in times of economic trouble.

Scientists now believe the world began with the "Big Bang", a definitive beginning. Some of them, even Albert Einstein, were reluctant to leave behind the theory that the universe was eternal, with no beginning, because the "Big Bang" theory was compatible with the Judaeo-Christian idea of God's creation.

Within that history of creation, God has also visited his people to confirm that human existence, with all its uncertainties, problems and suffering, has a deep meaning for everyone. Put quite simply, even for those in terrible circumstances, it is worth continuing to struggle, because God has demonstrated his interest in each one of us by coming among us, and by suffering as we sometimes do. Indeed he suffered more than most humans are called to suffer.

Jesus is the virtuous branch grown for David, foretold in Jeremiah. Therefore those who accept that the Son of God has come will be saved and will be able to dwell in confidence. Christians should be people of hope, aware of the triumphant conclusion to human history.

The resurrection of the dead, the resurrection both of the just and the unjust, will precede the Last Judgement. At that time all those who are in their tombs will hear the Son of Man's voice and come out and then Christ will come in his glory with all his angels for the separation, as a shepherd separates the sheep from the goats. Put in less rural language, we would say that in the presence of Christ, who is Truth himself, the truth of every person's relationship with God and therefore with one another, those manifold, mysterious relationships, will be laid bare.

That Last Judgement will occur when Christ returns in glory. Only the Father knows the day or the hour, only he will determine the moment of the coming. It seems certain that many of the early Christians thought that Christ would return quickly, so the Thessalonians stopped work and Paul had to tell them that that was not desirable, they had to stick at whatever they were doing. Saint Peter too explained the embarrassment, saying to people, *look, in God's eyes a thousand years are just like a day;* God will return in his own time.

The second coming is referred to as a liberation. God's justice will triumph over all the injustices committed by his creatures and we will have the final definitive proof that God's love is stronger than death. This message of the Last Judgement calls us to conversion, while God is still giving us the acceptable time; a time to repent and to believe and to try to do better.

After this Last Judgement, this final restoration, the righteous will reign forever with Christ, glorified in body and soul and also the universe itself will be renewed.

One of the consequences of the Incarnation, the Son of God becoming man, means that physical reality also is good, not just spiritual reality, and physical reality too will be taken up into what the Scriptures call this mysterious renewal, the new heavens and the new earth. That is also in Peter's letter.

It will be a definitive realisation of God's plan to bring under a single head everything in Christ, everything in heaven and everything on earth. It is sometimes described as the heavenly Jerusalem; God's dwelling amongst good people.

For all people this final consummation will be the ultimate realisation of the unity of the human race. We believe that the Catholic Church, which has to preach its message to every people and in a large measure has done this already, is a sacrament, a sign or a symbol of that final unity of all the redeemed around Christ. All those good people, and we hope we belong to them, will form the community of the redeemed, sometimes called the holy city of God, the new Jerusalem, the bride, the wife of the Lamb. And for the cosmos, as I mentioned, the whole immensity of the universe, there is this profound common destiny of the vindication of the material world.

Paul told us in the letter to the Romans that now the whole of creation is groaning in travail together until that time of restoration. We know, we are vividly aware sometimes more strongly than others, of sufferings and terrible evil and battles.

Eventually, at the end of time, the very world itself will be at the service not just of the Almighty God and his Son and the Spirit, but at the service of the just. So far from diminishing our concern about what is happening in this life, the expectancy that all our efforts will be taken up and transformed into the next life should give an extra impetus to our ordinary everyday work. The work of the kingdom of God is not exactly the same as earthly progress, but genuine human progress is a vital concern of the kingdom of God and it should be a consolation that our own personal achievements, when they are genuinely worthwhile, somehow will be taken up into the mystery of the new heaven and the new earth.

A very obvious example of that is the work of parents with their children. The good example and the love that they give is carried on for generations and generations and carried on also into eternity. When we spread on earth the fruits of our nature and our enterprise we hope and pray that in the next life we will find our families once again, cleansed this time from the stain of sin, illuminated and transfigured by Christ's redemptive action.

For this final consummation it is important that we follow the correct paths. So in today's Psalm we pray that the Lord may teach us his paths; may we find these paths to the truth and may we have the strength and persistence to follow them and not to be enticed off these paths by the many voices that will come to us. We need to stay awake, pray regularly, avoid drunkenness and debauchery, so we are blameless when the Lord comes.

The Rule of St. Benedict, the man who founded Western monasticism in the sixth century, sums it up nicely: "Run while you have the light, lest the darkness overtake you."

"A Baptism of Repentance for the Forgiveness of Sins"

2ND SUNDAY OF ADVENT
Baruch 5:1-9; Phil 1:4-6, 8-11; Gospel: Luke 3:1-6.

The basic point of Advent preparations for Christmas is to remind us of the enormous advantages we have because God has visited us by sending His Son among us, to teach us, to live with us and suffer like us, as He redeemed us. But an important by-product of Advent is that we are reminded of our present responsibilities, our duty not to drive Christ out of our hearts by sin and hatred and of the ultimately important fact that we shall meet Christ in death even before Christ returns in glory on the last day.

Both the Old Testament writer Baruch and St. Luke in his gospel as he quotes the Old Testament prophet Isaiah are working hard with their language to impress on their readers the enormous importance of the coming of God.

Jerusalem will be restored and faithful Jews will return from every corner of the world to celebrate the triumph. Jerusalem will be cloaked with integrity, which is necessary for the Godly triumph, dressed in beauty with a crown of glory. Their motto forever will be "peace through integrity and honour through devotedness".

We are now used to the marvels that our engineers have been able to accomplish for decades. Sydney is a city of skyscrapers; we have the Sydney Harbour Bridge and the elegant Anzac Bridge.

If we drive north on the M3 we can see how the engineers have cut through the mountains and built fantastic bridges across the valleys and the occasional river like the Hawkesbury. Such is the technological expertise available today they don't generally have to fill the valleys to avoid the hills which exhausted the horses, camels and those travelling by foot in ancient times. Such is the power of our cars, trucks and trains that they can easily surmount even steep inclines.

So it was from a different level of technological expertise that the Book of Baruch, whose earlier sections date from the sixth century B.C., spoke of God flattening the high mountains and the everlasting hills and filling the valleys to ground level. In those days all this was beyond their capacity except in a few limited situations, where slave labour substituted for modern machinery.

The passage from Isaiah which Luke quotes probably predates Baruch, as it runs a series of similar images. But in Isaiah's case it is a voice crying in the wilderness, which announces the good news. Then as now many were too busy to listen, even when they were sympathetic to the idea generally and of course a goodly percentage would have rejected as ridiculous any suggestion that all mankind would see the salvation of God.

John the Baptist, the son of priest Zachary and Elizabeth cousin of Our Lady was born 6 months before Jesus. Luke's Gospel tells us Gabriel the Archangel appeared to Zachary in the temple announcing that Elizabeth would conceive a son and telling him to give his promised son the name of John, which means "Yahweh is gracious". He would lead many of the sons of Israel to their Lord and would walk in the power and spirit of Elijah. In his canticle called the *Bendedictus*, Zachary sings of his son as "prophet of the Most High". According to tradition John was born in the town of Ain Karim, about five kilometres west of Jerusalem. Luke also relates that John spent his youth in the desert.

John appeared in the region of the Jordan as an ascetic and a preacher of penance. His principal task was to announce the arrival of Jesus Christ as Messiah and he in fact baptised Jesus. He appeared clothed in camel's hair, the traditional garb of the prophets; just as Elijah had.

John came as "a voice crying in the desert" echoing Isaiah. According to the Fourth Gospel the Baptist categorically denied that he was Elijah or the expected Prophet or the Messiah. But he was indeed the last of the Old Testament prophets.

The message of John's sermons is rather forbidding and severe (Mt 3.7-12; Mk 1.7-8; Lk3.7-18): "the axe is laid to the root of the trees". But Luke insists also on the positive and humane aspects of the Baptist's message. No profession is denied salvation; all are called primarily to practise justice and charity toward their fellow man.

In John's Gospel the Baptist describes himself as the friend of the Bridegroom who must decrease as Christ must increase; he proclaims Jesus as the Lamb of God.

John gathered around him a group of disciples who remained faithful to him until his death, including the apostles Andrew and John who had been his disciples before joining Christ. The Synoptic Gospels and John record disputes between the disciples of the Baptist and those of Christ over fasting and baptism. The Baptist, however, counselled his disciples to follow Jesus.

The Evangelists further describe how "all the country of Judaea went out to him, and all the inhabitants of Jerusalem". Josephus the ancient Jewish historian as well as the Evangelists, record the reaction of Herod Antipas, who, fearing an uprising, had the Baptist imprisoned. John had fearlessly denounced Herod's sinful marriage with Herodias, his brother's wife. In turn, Herodias instigated her daughter Salome to request John's death; to please her Herod had John beheaded, although he had regarded him as a religious and just man. While in prison, John had sent a delegation of his disciples to ask Jesus if He was the Messiah. According to some critics, John had found it difficult to accept a meek and merciful Messiah rather than an Elijah-like figure. In answer, Jesus pointed to his fulfilment of the Old Testament messianic expectation, especially as described by Isaiah. He then took the occasion to eulogise John as "a prophet, yes, more than a prophet ... Among those born of women there has not arisen a greater than John the Baptist".

The Dead Sea scrolls were discovered by a shepherd boy in 1947. They had belonged to the Qumran Community, probably a Jewish group called the Essenes.

Many scholars believe that the Qumran community of the Judean desert had an important influence on the Baptist. Some claim that John belonged to the community for a while and I am inclined to believe this.

These similarities are striking, e.g., that of the messianic expectation of the Judean desert. The Qumran community was a priestly one; John, too, came from a priestly family that manifested intense messianic hopes. Both John and the sectarians of Qumran found inspiration in the text of Isaiah 40.3 about a voice crying in the wilderness to prepare the way of the Lord. John preached a baptism of repentance, and while the Qumran community practised ritual ablutions, there is no indication that they attached any moral significance to these. While the Qumran ritual was frequently repeated, that of John was apparently administered only once. John announced a second baptism with the Holy Spirit and with fire, that is, an eschatological judgement; the Qumran ascetics, too, preached a second baptism that would be the work of the Spirit of God and would be eschatological.

A striking difference, however, between John the Baptist and the Qumran community is the universality present in John's preaching in contrast to the closed character of the Qumran group, which regarded all outsiders as "sons of darkness."

John's call to repentance and therefore forgiveness is as necessary now as it was 2000 years ago, but until the discovery of the scrolls in the Qumran monastery the plausibility of the young John living for years in the wilderness or desert was always open to challenge.

Modern studies have filled out the background of this exotic figure. All believers are in the debt of these scholars.

The last of the Old Testament prophets was a precursor to the greatest of all the prophets, Jesus Christ, the Word of God in person, speaking in our midst.

"What must we do?"
3RD SUNDAY OF ADVENT
Zeph 3:14-18; Phil 4:4-7;
Gospel: Luke 3:10-18.

These readings for the third Sunday of Advent have the dual message of Advent loud and clear. First of all we should rejoice, because of the marvellous event which is approaching. The psalm's refrain is "Cry out with joy and gladness: for among you is the great and Holy One of Israel". Paul also wants us to be happy in the Lord so that the peace of God guards our hearts and thoughts.

Zephaniah put it a bit differently, and sometimes a bit too aggressively. "The Lord, the king of Israel, is in your midst, you have no more evil to fear." A few lines further on he describes the Lord who has driven Israel's enemies away as a "victorious warrior".

This harks back to the suspicion of some scholars that John the Baptist was expecting a fierce Messiah like Elijah of old and helps explain the general mindset of the Jews then which was scandalised by the prospect of the Messiah dying on a cross: and probably by a Messiah being born in a stable.

The second part of the Advent message is encapsulated in the request of the people to John the Baptist. "What must we do?" now that the Messiah is coming.

First of all John insisted that they help those without clothes and those who are hungry. Then "do your duty" he explained to the different categories of person: the comfortable, the tax collectors, the soldiers. Tax collectors and soldiers were not popular with the Jews but neither was subjected to a blanket rejection. They were both told not to take advantage of others to rob them. All are called to follow the Messiah, who is not John himself. "I am not fit to undo the strap of his sandals," he explained vividly.

We too are called to repent and believe; to do our duty in our respective and immensely different tasks or vocations. If you believe you are in your correct niche, whatever your task, homemaker, student, employee or employer; if you believe God has a plan for each one of us, for you, then that is a vocation.

Generally, and quite properly, the accent is on interior renewal, on preparing our hearts to celebrate Christ's birth. This is one consequence of the long-term significance of the Incarnation. Jesus' coming is not like the visit of a much loved grandparent, aunt or uncle to a family of young children. Often the children are delighted and excited by such a visit, but the visitors leave and then life goes on with parents and children.

According to John the Baptist, the Messiah's visit is different. "His winnowing-fan is in his hand to clear his threshing-floor and gather the wheat into his barn; but the chaff he will burn in a fire that will never go out." Jesus' coming is a challenge, which provokes change of one kind or another with long-term consequences. This is not the type of challenge many of the Jews were anticipating; this was a new type of baptism with the Holy Spirit.

However I want to conclude these few Advent musings, not by concentrating on our heart of hearts, but on our external and even public activities. Generally what is in our hearts is expressed publicly; in turn these external activities reinforce our inner convictions. Do we regularly give any sign that we have received the Good News, that we know about Christ's redemptive activity, and are grateful for the Maker's instructions?

How often and in what ways do we give public expression to our faith, to our membership of the Catholic Church?

Let us start with Christmas. When we choose our Christmas cards, do we insist on cards which reflect the Incarnation, rather than Santa, or reindeers, or an Australian bush scene?

Do we wish people a happy Christmas or simply "Season's greetings"? Do we erect a crib in our house?

In fact when people come into our homes could they ever guess that we are Christians? Are there any Christian symbols, like a cross or crucifix, in our lounge rooms or at the entrance to our home? Do we urge the teenagers in our families that when they are decorating their bedrooms or study places that they should include a crucifix, perhaps a picture of Mary, mother of God; perhaps a portrait of a saint they admire?

Would we ever wear a cross around our neck, any visible personal sign of loyalty to Christ?

Inner convictions have to be externally manifested, expressed in community if they are to continue as real and effective, because we are made of body as well as soul, and our personality and our convictions are expressed through our actions.

This is one reason why we come together in community worship every Sunday for Mass, rather than claiming that we pray/meditate quietly at home as an alternative. This is why we have marriage ceremonies, as the spouses publicly proclaim their love to one another. It is part of the rationale for all the sacraments, because we are community persons of flesh and blood. This public dimension is one reason why individual confession and priestly absolution are so important.

On most Christmases there is a mild flutter as persons like myself urge publicly that we keep Christ in Christmas. That is why we have the crib in the square before the Cathedral and more public Christmas decorations than in the past. We should get serious and do some long-term planning to encourage this. But we cannot blame businesses too much, especially businesses run by non-Christians or ex-Christians, for their failings in this matter, if we never advertise personally our own Catholicism.

Would our workmates, or friends at university know that we are Catholic? In conversation are we prepared to defend and explain the Catholic position on controversial issues?

I have asked many questions, which we might describe as Advent questions, prompted by our public celebrations of the birth of the Son of God.

People with something to sell or share, know that it is important to advertise. A good cause needs to be publicised.

If we are never prepared, or rarely prepared, to advertise that we are Catholics, followers of Christ, what does this tell us of our inner convictions, about the quality of our faith? What would John the Baptist be exhorting us to do with the Good News?

"Blessed is the Fruit of Your Womb"

4TH SUNDAY OF ADVENT
Micah 5:1-4; Heb 10:5-10;
Gospel: Luke 1:39-44.

Almost on the eve of Christmas, we should retrace with the help of the readings some of the basics of the feast we are about to celebrate.

The future ruler of Israel was expected to come from Bethlehem, which was not a wealthy suburb of Jerusalem, not a playground for the rich, not the site of an elite school. It was home to the least of the clans of Judah and God was promising, in Micah's prophecy, to abandon his people until "she who is to give birth gives birth".

At Christmas we celebrate the birth of the man-God, who will become our redeemer. But especially now we should not forget the baby's mother, Mary, the principal actor/agent in the story, the one who had to do most of the work, with the help of her husband Joseph.

Catholics, Orthodox and many Anglicans and Protestants have great devotion to Jesus' mother but opposition to this devotion was a burning issue at the Reformation. Even today some Protestant groups have no public devotions to Mary.

This is a pity as Mary has a prominent place in the New Testament. She is "full of grace" and "all ages will call her blessed". In today's Gospel, Mary visits her cousin Elizabeth and is greeted thus: "of all women you are the most blessed and blessed is the fruit of your womb". But, in many ways Mary does not fit our conventional patterns.

Two thousand years ago Palestine was very different. There were no teenagers. Adolescence is a modern invention, like secondary education and today some, often rich and overeducated, can still be adolescent at 35. In those ancient days there was only a sudden transition, often brutal, between childhood and adult life.

In all probability Mary was like her contemporaries and gave birth to Jesus when she was thirteen or fourteen. The great French Catholic author Georges Bernanos described her as our young sister. The Scriptures also do not tell us anything about Joseph's age, but ancient traditions describe him as a much older man, and this is plausible.

Bible Christians of every denomination believe that Jesus was divine and had no human father. This is taught by the New Testament and believed in faith.

Sexual misbehaviour by women was then a capital offence, so it is not surprising that Joseph had decided to divorce his fiancée quietly when he discovered her pregnancy; before he was reassured in a dream.

All Jesus' natural characteristics came from his mother, although there is no doubt that the loving nurture of Joseph and the extended family contributed also.

The beauty of Jesus' character, his prayer and piety, his wisdom and strength, his charisma for leadership and courage would have been impossible without Mary's love, care and example; and her genes.

It is no coincidence that some of civilisation's greatest paintings (Da Vinci's "La Madonna Litta"; the Vladimir Madonna), sculptures

(Michelangelo's "Pieta") and music (the "Ave Maria" of Schubert or Bach and Gounod) are centred on Mary.

She was a woman of faith, grace and strength, who had a hard life, giving birth in a cave, later a political refugee in Egypt, who lived to see her son crucified.

Christians believe that only God is worthy of worship. Therefore Mary is not worshipped, but reverenced; prayed to as someone who has special influence with God. She points to God through her son, and is reverenced more as a model of faith and practice than as a mother.

The Catholic Church also teaches that Mary remained a virgin, despite the Scriptural references to "the brothers of Jesus", traditionally seen as cousins in the Western tradition. An Eastern and Orthodox tradition believes the brothers were Joseph's children from an earlier marriage!

The Catholic (i.e., Western & Eastern, Orthodox and Roman) devotion to Mary is one of the most wonderful Christian contributions to piety and culture.

Hardline feminists are generally hostile to Our Lady. I remember hearing a feminist Scripture scholar give a talk on women in the Scriptures and never mention, Mary, Mother of God. Not a bad effort!

I suppose they are opposed to the concept of virginity, perhaps opposed to giving respect to motherhood.

Another possible reason is found in the second reading where Christ announces that he has come to do God's will, just as Mary did at the visitation, when she consented to the Incarnation, announced that she would cooperate with God's plan. The new pagans love personal autonomy, refusing sub-ordination to anyone, even God.

Christmas should remind us, and especially Mary's cooperation should remind us that the most important task in life is to do God's will, initially at least by keeping the commandments. We are not here to do our own thing, write our own rules, disregard or hurt others, choose evil.

Sometimes, many times, it is hard to know which good option to choose, but our general direction, our basic option should be clear: to follow Christ and his mother Mary in their willingness to do God's will.

"The First Crib"
CHRISTMAS MIDNIGHT MASS (Sermon 1)
Isaiah 9:1-7; Titus 2:11-14;
Gospel: Luke 2:1-14.

Soon after Jesus' birth Mary and Joseph had to flee into exile in Egypt to escape being eliminated by King Herod, who feared the birth of a possible long-term rival. It is sad and disturbing that two thousand years later we still find no permanent peace in the Middle East. In a special way, therefore, we must join the Old Testament psalmist and "pray for the peace of Jerusalem".

At Christmas we should not only think of our families, but extend our sympathy more widely. We thank God for the peace we enjoy in Australia. We remember in prayer those who do not have peace in their hearts at this time, those who are sick, those who are lonely and estranged, those caught up in doing drugs, alcoholics, the homeless. May they be consoled by the beauty of Christmas as hundreds of millions of ordinary people have been, just as painters and poets, musicians and singers have been inspired for two thousand years. We first hear this in the poetry of St. Luke's gospel account of the birth of our Saviour – the census; the birth in a stable; the shepherds and the angels around "a baby wrapped in swaddling clothes and lying in a manger". Many great saints have preached on this text, such as St. Francis of Assisi to the people of Greccio, a remote mountain village in Italy, at Christmas in the year 1223.

St. Francis had prepared a manger in the small church, complete with a live cow and donkey, the first recorded crib in Christian history. As he spoke of the wonder of the Incarnation, the truth that the Son of God took on our human nature, his voice broke with emotion. The bystanders claimed they saw a child in the straw, who was raised from a deep sleep by Francis' words. There was a lesson here, because the Child Jesus had been forgotten by many. Who could claim that it is much different today in Australia?

Christmas again warms our hearts with the fundamental truth of our faith. Jesus is Emmanuel, God-with-us. In the baby asleep in the hay, the believer perceives a two-fold reality, first of all a newborn child, humanity at its most helpless. At the same time, the believer can see the beautiful face of the Almighty and Invisible God.

It is wonderful that God chose to come among us in this way and not even as the son of rich or powerful parents. Every birth is the unfolding of a great mystery, a cause for wonder and gratitude, especially for the parents, but also for all family and friends.

This surely is where Christianity stands alone. In the poor stable of Bethlehem, we stand at the point of intersection between the divine and the human. No one can say, "God became one of us" unless prompted by faith. No one can acknowledge the birth of the Son of God without gratitude.

The Spirit of Christmas gives both light and life. If we do not believe, we remain in the dark, where there is so much doubt and sadness. It is the land of deep shadow, a land of heavy burdens, of struggling under the rod of the oppressor. Christmas is a call to believe and Catholics must actively welcome the increasing number of Australians who are searching for love and meaning. The old sectarian hostilities among Christians are almost entirely gone. We thank God for this, although secular hostility has increased.

This Christmas, as we visit the crib, and see and hear the story again, we should ask ourselves: "How is my faith? Do I believe that God became man in Jesus?" To believe this is to step away from the shadows and illusions into the world of God, where the light of faith gives healing and purpose. When Christ was born, a star illuminated the night. That same star still sheds its peaceful light on all of human life, our hopes and sorrows, our dreams and fears. We are all called to follow that star.

With a firm belief in the Incarnation, there can be greater peace and goodwill among people. With the conviction that God is with us, the unquiet heart will know true rest. One of the great difficulties of our modern age, and for many Christians too, is that we only half believe. We do not go the whole way and say with conviction "I believe" in God made man.

The Australian poet Les Murray wrote recently that if we drop Christ from Christmas, this summer festival could become a powerful, even dangerous dream, a short-cut version of heaven on earth, which ignores death and the impossibility of equality and justice.

Christians confront this in the knowledge that the Incarnation is completed by the Crucifixion, where the Christ Child grew up, took the blame for our crimes and sins, died and rose again to show that life and love and justice will have the last word.

In this third Christian millennium, let us ask the Christ child to deepen in us the faith necessary to believe those impossible and embarrassing truths. As Les Murray's proposed epitaph puts it, "Impossibility is the only door that opens".

"Christmas Gifts"

CHRISTMAS MIDNIGHT MASS (Sermon 2)
Isaiah 9:1-7; Titus 2:11-14;
Gospel: Luke 2:1-14.

I always have resisted those who suggest that Father Christmas is hostile to our Christian understanding of the feast. He is a bit of a "Johnny come lately", created by Coca Cola in an advertising campaign in the 1920s, but his prototype was St. Nicholas from Turkey in the fourth century A.D., a bishop renowned for the practical help he gave to battlers and specially for the dowries he provided for three young sisters which enabled them to be married and saved them from a life of prostitution.

I hope that this type of charity is not needed among us today, but the general Christian message is clear; that at Christmas we should be thinking of others, especially those who could do with a helping hand, and not thinking of ourselves. Christmas is God thinking of us.

Recently I had dinner with a group which included a duchess from Europe. She grew up in a good Catholic family and she spoke lovingly of her father, who had a strong faith and was also a wise and loving husband and father. As they were rich, the children always had many Christmas presents, but before opening them each had to choose three to give to the poor. I am sure this caused some heartburn to the children, but it was a lesson that woman never forgot. It captures something of the real spirit of Christmas.

It is good to try to identify what we, what the Catholic Church celebrates at Christmas. As a first step the feast clearly teaches us that human existence has a meaning beyond the material facts of life. Money is a means to either good or bad ends; it is not a value in itself. Money and possessions cannot return your love and in the long run money cannot do much against personal suffering and cannot beat death, although it can delay it.

Man is a religious animal and if we do not choose a religion like Christianity, which only comes at some cost, we shall probably be embracing cheap substitutes, easy superstitions.

The Christian message is clear and provocative. Human life has truth and meaning, so much so that our loving God sent his Son to share our human condition; the highs and the lows and the humdrum.

You do not need to be a duchess or a professor to understand this. You do not even need to be a believer to be moved by the idea of God being among us as a baby in a stable, as a young man crucified on a cross.

For those of us who believe such claims, the Christian message can be ennobling and regularly brings strength and consolation.

The feast of Christmas will outlive all of its commercial rivals and in fact business needs Christmas. No market will be sustained in the long term by selfish people buying presents for themselves!

Christmas is a time for others and especially Christmas is a time for God – a time to thank Almighty God – the transcendent Lord of human history, the creator of the universe, the guiding hand, the Intelligent Designer behind all the developments we can explain by evolution and those we cannot yet explain – to thank God Almighty for sending his Son among us, to teach us and redeem us.

Those who accept and understand the Christ Child have genuine insight into God himself, into God's love and wisdom. This is the message of Christmas.

Every peace and blessing to you and yours at this Christmas time.

"Not an Eternal Cycle of Return"

NEW YEAR'S DAY MASS – MARY MOTHER OF GOD

Num 6:22-27; Gal 4:4-7;
Gospel: Luke 2:16-21

"When the appointed time came, God sent his Son, born of a woman, to redeem the subjects of the Law and to enable us to be adopted as sons and daughters. No longer are we slaves".

That is Saint Paul writing to the Galatians not long after the middle of the first Christian century. That is what we celebrate at every Christmas. And this is what will sustain us and those who follow us in the third Christian millennium.

Christianity has a culture of remembrance played out in the many different feasts and seasons of the liturgical year; Lent, Easter, Pentecost, then eventually back to Advent and Christmas.

We are not celebrating the transitory news in the headlines; news which will be stale tomorrow. We celebrate lasting achievements, full of promise for tomorrow; the Incarnation and Redemption. God has blessed us in his mercy, because God has spoken to us through his Son, not simply through saints and prophets.

The Christian religion changed the way the Western world looks at time. For the ancient Greeks, like the Buddhists and Hindus today, all life goes in an endless cycle. These great Asian religions talk of reincarnation. If your lot is miserable in this life, you were evil in a former life. It is one approach to the problem of evil and suffering. There is nothing new under the sun, only the everlasting return of the seasons, of day and night.

We do not believe in an everlasting cycle of return. The Jews introduced time's arrow into popular thinking. They were and are waiting for the Messiah, not the only Son of God, who redeemed us and pointed us to the last days, his Second Coming for the last and final judgement.

Christianity does not only look backward. It celebrates and thanks God for Catholic and Christian vitality today and points forward in hope to the rewards of heaven in the next life.

We humans have to confront our fears. Our faith in Christ brings consolation, which develops into Christian hope, quite unlike the pessimism of some secularists, centred on things such as nuclear war, ecological disaster and over-population.

We hope for salvation beyond history; an escape into heaven, emerging from darkness into the light of total revelation, to see God face to face. Eternal bliss is completely different from reincarnation where we start again and again and again, with no hope of escape, only improvement.

Life is difficult and complicated, like mazes at some medieval cathedrals. There is no Christian teaching that life must get better as we progress through history. It is impossible to transform the world definitively. No gains are complete and no gains are permanent. It is much better, and closer to Christian teaching, to love those close to us and make what improvements we can there. It is a necessary beginning. Nostalgia for a lost paradise or the impossible hope of rediscovering on earth a lost paradise is a dead end.

The United States author Tom Wolfe once spoke of the hippies in San Francisco in the 1960s and 70s starting from zero and sweeping away all restraints; so they rediscovered the ancient diseases which had disappeared. They paid the price.

There are truths to be known and found in the person and teachings of Jesus. The heart and the cause for rejoicing was that life has meaning because suffering has meaning, which we cannot understand in time, but which Christ has promised can bring fruit and will be balanced out in eternity.

History will finish well, except for the adamantly evil and those who refuse to ask for pardon, because Christian life is like a difficult pilgrimage to a holy state or place. It is a promise of better things; something radically better, i.e., God.

So we thank God for the blessing of the past year. We thank God too that we survived the twentieth century – the worst and best in history. We look forward to the Christian future.

My prayer for you is the prayer the Lord gave to Moses –

May the Lord bless you and keep you.
May the Lord let his face shine on you and be gracious to you.
May the Lord uncover his face to you and bring you his peace.

"Many Problems"
THE HOLY FAMILY
Sirach 3:2-6, 12-14; Col 3:12-21;
Gospel: Luke 2:41-52.

The feast of the Holy Family is always an occasion to meditate on the central importance of the family and to draw consolation from the difficulties they faced.

We know about the major difficulties in the life of Mary and Joseph; the mysterious pregnancy, no suitable accommodation, the flight into Egypt, many refusing to accept Jesus' teaching, the opposition and abuse he provoked, his untimely death. These are great and dramatic difficulties; worthy obstacles for the first family of history in the struggle between good and evil.

But we can be tempted to think that the Holy Family avoided the smaller unseemly tensions and mishaps of family life. For example, some family friends of mine went camping just before Christmas. While they were there they were hit by two terrible storms. It took them six hours to put up the tents after the youngest child in the family broke the central support pole. As the oldest child said to me, they all had at least sixty fights when they were away on their camping expedition.

Jesus being lost in the Temple at Jerusalem shows the Holy Family probably had their share of lesser problems, of misunderstandings. Mary said, when they found Jesus, "Why have you done this? Joseph and I were terribly worried." We are told simply they did not understand Jesus' reply that he had to be about his Father's business.

We must be convinced of the importance of the family and we must pray for our own families constantly and regularly and we must pray for the institution of the family in our society. There are immense changes taking place in family life, not just through the increase in divorce although that is very significant, but because people are living longer and having fewer children. In our newspapers we still hear writers moralising solemnly about the problems of over-population in Asia and South America, while in fact our own situation is absolutely the reverse. There is no country in the Western world which is producing enough children to keep the population levels stable. Some countries are already in serious population decline, such as Russia. So the contrast between the local situation and the theorising is actually quite bizarre!

I remember once reading a book which had been given to me called, *Conversations about the End of Time*. One of the contributors was Umberto Eco, an Italian atheist and a fine writer. He is sometimes dubbed a "Catholic atheist" because he recognises the indispensable contribution of Catholicism to Western civilisation although he does not believe. His best-known book written in the 1980s is called *The Name of the Rose* and was made into a film. This is a great read. In the "Conversations" Eco predicted that population pressures would force the Western world to follow the Chinese pattern and limit children to one child per family, even alleging that the notions of a sister and a brother would be buried in the collective memory, just like fairies in childhood stories! He claimed that in the future it would be difficult to explain to a child what it means to love a sister or brother. He might have been writing in this way to produce hostile reactions like my own!

May God preserve our Australian society and any society from such a fate. May God always preserve Australian Catholic communities from such a fate. Children are God's gift, signs of God's blessing. Married couples in the Christian and Catholic view have solemn obligations to continue the human race; children are the fruit of their love for one another. Even if the human family, living at the same time across four generations becomes more common, families with only one child as the norm would be a spiritual disaster. Brothers and sisters in a loving family are usually better at teaching one another to be unselfish than even their parents.

More and more people in China are coming to resist their draconian policy of only one child per family. Already there is a surplus of young men, perhaps in tens of millions, given the hostility to having a daughter as an only child. On top of this the balance between productive workers and dependents is shifting disastrously. China and indeed India will follow European patterns in a generation or so and become top-heavy with the elderly. But, unlike Europe, they will become old before all their people are rich.

The Old Testament obligations of parents and children towards one another, which we heard about in the first Reading from the book of Ecclesiasticus, remain in place. Obedience and respect from children towards their parents usually bring rewards in this life too. The kindness of children to their fathers and mothers, as the book of Ecclesiasticus says, will serve as reparation for sins. Children have obligations to support their parents in their old age – not put them in a home and then leave them unvisited except at Christmas and Easter!

A sense of humour helps. On this lighter note, I am reminded of a poster on a car window, which said, "Take revenge! Live long enough to be a worry to your children".

Our families will always be better families if, as Saint Paul urged the Colossians, we "let the message of Christ, in all its richness, find a home" in our families.

Regular prayer in families is essential, not just Sunday Mass, and regular efforts at compassion, kindness, patience and forgiveness. These cannot be learned too young and the young learn more from our example as adults than from all our preaching.

One final word. It is a reasonable expectation that governments, and therefore the law, protect and privilege the institution of marriage, which produces long term benefits to society. We should combat those proposing legislation to give equal legal status and protection to homosexual unions. I am not advocating homophobia; I believe deeply in tolerance and justice and justice too for surviving partners of whatever sort of liaison there might have been, but the laws must respect and must recognise and protect the central role of the family. If we depart from that, those coming after us, I believe, will pay an increasing price.

"Baptism of the Lord"

1ST SUNDAY IN ORDINARY TIME
Isaiah 42:1-4, 6-7; Acts 10:34-38;
Gospel: Luke 3:15-6.21-2.

At this time of year the situation moves quickly in the cycle during the liturgical year which commemorates the events in Our Lord's life.

We recently celebrated the feast of the Epiphany remembering the visit of the wise men from the East to the baby Jesus, anticipating the universal message of salvation which Christ would announce.

Today we have moved on nearly thirty years to the feast of the Baptism of Our Lord, a ceremony which occurred as Jesus was about to commence his public life.

Baptism, a blessing accompanied by the pouring of water over the head or by the immersion in water of the person to be baptised, was not a mainstream Jewish celebration, although one group of Jews called the Essenes had ritual washings with water in their monasteries as they struggled to purify their hearts. John the Baptist probably spent some time with them as a child and young man, because the Jewish ascetics took in young recruits to live with them and it was John's practice of baptism, which he conferred on his followers, which Jesus received and the Church adopted in its sacrament of baptism. However for John the Baptist and for the Church baptism can only be conferred once, distinguishing it from the regular ceremonies of the Essenes.

We find brief accounts of Our Lord's baptism in the gospels of Matthew, Mark and Luke, where all agree that John was the celebrant, that Jesus was immersed in the Jordan river, and that the event was accompanied by a theophany, where the Spirit of God in the form of a dove appeared, announcing that Jesus was God's beloved Son and that God's favour rested upon him.

In faith we are all called to believe that God has a plan for each one of us, which we should endeavour to recognise and embrace by accepting what we call our "vocation". God has to be adaptable, because having the gift of free will we sometimes sin and sometimes don't listen for God's call; or more rarely, reject what we suspect God might be wanting for us. Priests, brothers and nuns are not the only people with vocations as every person fits into God's plan.

With billions of people in the world today and billions who have gone before us and billions more to come, a Godly plan for each of us seems too much even for God! The prodigious capacity of giant computers to store and rearrange billions of pieces of information, a human invention, throws new light on God's capacity to be interested in each one of us. I was also struck by the ability of the English author J.R. Tolkien, in his huge novel *The Lord of the Rings*, to bring together all the struggles, misfortunes and mistakes of his characters to the desired conclusion. For some reason, not entirely clear to me, this helped me better appreciate the reality of God's providence for each one of us.

God obviously had special plans for his only Son Jesus, but where does this baptism fit? Why it was necessary or appropriate for Jesus to be baptised?

Most of the commentators associate the baptism with Jesus' claim that he was the Messiah, the leader who the Jews were expecting to come and provide political and religious leadership for them.

We are told that while there was no single image of the Messiah throughout the Jewish community in Jesus' day, being the Messiah was not seen as a claim to divinity.

But the concept of the Messiah was linked to the Temple and Jewish royalty so that it was expected this public figure would struggle against and defeat evil, bring back Israel politically or symbolically from exile and reinstate God in Zion; vindicate the universal claims of the one true God.

Our Lord was not a simple country lad with the four evangelists as spin doctors and Paul in particular as the theoretician and strategist who directed the propaganda campaign. Jesus was the most profound theologian, original and subtle, who won over the New Testament writers and provided them through his teaching and activities with the foundations for their theologising.

Our Lord believed that God's kingdom and Israel's destiny were fulfilled through him; he was to fight Israel's battles and a new religious community or identity would be forged around him. This was his conviction long before his suffering and death, although he could not announce it too soon or too clearly because it would cause trouble with both civic and religious authorities and provoke misleading political hopes among many of the people.

Through symbolic actions such as his driving the money changers from the Temple and his triumphal entry into Jerusalem, Jesus claimed the Messiah-ship.

But equally importantly, he pointed to his baptism by John to legitimise his claims. John was the last of the prophets who announced the One, who was the Saviour. Jesus' baptism by John confirmed this.

We cannot enter into the psychology of Jesus at this point. We cannot pinpoint the mysterious workings of his divine and human natures to say whether he received God's call and recognised it at that stage or that the ceremony was only a public confirmation of the special call He had long acknowledged. Jesus' life and ministry exemplify human developments while the interaction with his divine nature is shrouded in mystery.

What is true is that the Jewish prophecies were fulfilled in a paradoxical way by Jesus the Messiah. He did not restore the Temple or free Israel from the Romans, but he broke the power of evil and established a new Kingdom of God on earth and in heaven.

"The Spirit of the Lord is Upon Me"
3RD & 4TH SUNDAYS IN ORDINARY TIME
Neh 8:2-6, 8-10; 1 Cor 12:12-30;
Gospel: Luke 1:1-4, 4:14-30.

In 598 B.C. the Jewish kingdom was defeated by the Babylonians, Jerusalem was destroyed and the Jewish people taken into exile in Babylon. Today in Jerusalem deep under the city we can see the excavated walls and gate where the Babylonians entered the city.

Happily for the Jews, Cyrus the King of Persia defeated the Babylonians sixty years later in 538 and allowed the remnant, those Jews who wanted to return, to go to Jerusalem now part of the Persian Empire.

Life was difficult although the temple was rebuilt fairly quickly, but one hundred years later the walls of Jerusalem still had not been rebuilt, the gates were ruined and the Jewish people dispirited and in disarray.

Two Jews were responsible for improving the situation, the first being Nehemiah, a layman, who obtained permission from the Persian King Artaxerxes to return to Jerusalem with government money to rebuild the city and especially the walls This was in 445 B.C. The other leader was Ezra the priest who restored the Jewish religion around the ancient book of the Law.

In the reading from Nehemiah we hear of a solemn gathering of all the devout to hear the Law read to them – a long session from the crack of dawn to midday. The people were weeping, but not from boredom or exhaustion; they prostrated themselves because they realised the beauty and usefulness of this Godly teaching.

Ezra ordered a feast because "the joy of the Lord is your strength".

Psalm 18 explains the significance of God's teaching for the Jews of 2,500 years ago and for us as Christians today. The words of the Lord give spirit and life; his law is perfect, his witness is true, the commands are just and give light to the eyes. We are able to understand the difficulties and predicament of life through God's teachings. The Lord is our rock and our redeemer.

The history of God's special people extends for more than 3,500 years, including 2,000 years of Christianity. On many occasions during this time people have lost their way. Here and there the faith has died, but again and again individuals have recognised the light and whole communities have returned to the way of life and truth. The people listening to Ezra wept because they understood this.

With the coming of Jesus this history of salvation reached a new and definitive stage and Luke began his gospel by explaining to Theophilus that after examining the evidence he wanted to set out an ordered account of Jesus' life and teaching.

In these verses of Luke today we hear of another incident in the Holy Land, 450 years after Ezra, when Jesus the preacher returned to his own village of Nazareth to read the Old Testament scriptures, the word of God. In Galilee everyone knew of him already because after his time in the desert he had begun to teach in the region.

Jesus is the Servant of God described by Isaiah. Then, as today he had a happy message for the poor, freedom for prisoners, not only the prisoners in gaol, but prisoners to hate, drugs, pornography. Also he gives sight to the blind, not only the physically blind, but to all those who are confused, do not understand the meaning of life and are without hope. In all those ways God's teaching, through Jesus, frees the oppressed.

I had always thought of the Nazareth synagogue, (where the locals gathered to read the Law and hear the commandments) as holding 100 to 150 people. Contemporary scholarship suggests that it would only have held about 30 people, which is the size of a synagogue in the Nazareth of Jesus' time which the Christians of Nazareth have now reconstructed for us.

But it was still a dramatic moment in this small building. The young local was claiming to be the Servant of God described in Isaiah. All eyes were on him. "Today the Scripture which you have heard with your own ears is fulfilled" he announced.

So far so good, as the locals were initially delighted at his gracious words. However the mood changed quickly, when he responded to their demands for miracles like those he performed in Capernaum, by explaining that "no prophet is acceptable in his own country" and that both Elijah and Elisha performed their miracles away from home.

The locals were furious and wanted to kill him, but he slipped away from them.

From these earliest preaching days Jesus provoked rejection as well as acceptance, a feature He shares with the Church He founded. One writer even claimed that opposition and persecution constitute a fifth sign or mark of the true Church, which must be one, holy, apostolic and Catholic, which means "universal" in Greek, and attacked.

It is easy to sympathise with the locals, who knew Jesus as a baby, then as a boy. They would have known Mary and Joseph, his uncles and aunts and his cousins.

Already there was tension between Jesus' family at Nazareth and his group of disciples. Many in his family were jealous of the disciples, wanted to see miracles and believed that they too should receive them, simply because they were family and friends, who had known Jesus since he was a boy. They did not realise that faith is always necessary as in the days of Ezra, and in our time.

And it can be difficult for us too in moments of darkness to believe that this young man from Nazareth is the only Son of God, the Eternal Word, not just a prophet or a poet. We thank God for the gift of faith.

"Called"

5TH SUNDAY IN ORDINARY TIME
Isaiah 6:1-8; 1Cor 15:1-11;
Gospel: Luke 5:1-11.

The lake of Gennesaret is still one of the most beautiful spots in the Holy Land and I find it consoling that Our Lord liked to go there.

2000 years ago the lake was much larger and levels today fluctuate not only with the rains, but with the amount of water taken for irrigation.

From the first century Jewish historian Josephus we know that the surrounding countryside was then covered with lush vegetation and a variety of wild animals roamed there. It was probably even more beautiful than it is today.

As always we must remember that Our Lord was and is true man as well as true God and I find consolation not only in the fact that he worked and preached around this lake, but that he loved this area and used it for prayer and quiet.

In this incident we have Jesus stepping into one of the fishing boats to address the crowd which was pressing around him.

When he finished his teaching he, a carpenter and preacher, asked the fishermen who had caught nothing all night to head out into the lake and try again. Peter was no fool, probably one of the most successful local fishermen, someone who knew his business. He would have done as he was asked by this strange gentleman, whom he addresses as "master", but only out of respect and politeness.

They then caught so many fish that their boats were in danger of sinking.

Peter realised immediately that this was no ordinary fishing expedition. He was in the presence of the divine, of God at work in his creation. His was a typical action for a God-fearing Jew. Jesus was no longer addressed as master but as "Lord", Peter confessed his own inadequacy and sinfulness and asked to be left alone, for Jesus to leave. Peter fell at his feet in reverence.

Two more surprises followed. Jesus immediately asked Peter and the brothers James and John (but not Andrew, Peter's brother – at least in Luke's version) to leave their fishing and join him in preaching and teaching to become "fishers of men". The second surprise was that they did as they were asked: "they left everything and followed him".

What would we leave to follow Christ? What sacrifices would we make to remain faithful?

Do we truly think of knowing Christ, of knowing the basics of Catholic tradition as a great advantage? Do we take it for granted? Has it become simply a matter of habit? Do we think of it as our way of looking at things, one way among many? Is coming to know and follow Christ like coming into the light?

Those of us who are healthy should be aware of this blessing and thank God for it. Do we think of our faith in the way we think of our health? Like the advantages of education, or the ability to get away for holidays?

Faith is more important in our lives than any of these. It is the secret to life after death, it gives a purpose and meaning to our ordinary lives. We know God; we have someone to turn to in time of trouble.

Sometimes good people without faith better realise the treasure we have. Our view of faith can be like our view of our own family! Sometimes youngsters do not appreciate how good it was with their parents until they leave home, or have to build a marriage and look after their own children, or see the suffering in many families.

Many things are needed to sustain a strong community of faith: good families, schools, strong laity, mutual help and priests. Probably the single greatest need of the church in the next 25 years is for more priests. I am not pessimistic on this score. Vocations have always been somewhat scarce. I think we have passed the bottom of the trough.

There are three points we should keep in mind:

- Priesthood is a great life and not a refuge for those who cannot make it in the wider world. It holds many consolations, attracts great support from many people, and many opportunities for service and leadership in faith.
- We should regularly pray for vocations. A priestly vocation is a mystery of faith, and the crucial element is the faith dimension. Altruism is expressed in many ways. I still suspect many are called but do not answer, that God continues to call but too many are tuned to a different wave length.
- We should also actively support those who are thinking of priesthood. I am sometimes surprised by the number of good practising Catholics who are hostile to the idea of someone going off to try a vocation to priesthood. Some people are in favour of vocations, provided they come from somewhere else! Popular esteem of priests

and priesthood is an important factor in whether young men will consider priesthood as a vocation and we thank God that the drought of vocations to the priesthood in Australia has eased in many dioceses.

After praying for priests, successors to Peter and Andrew, James and John, we should not forget that God calls all Christians to cooperate in his personal plan for them, which respects our freedom to say yes, no or maybe. Human response is the major reason why God writes straight in crooked lines as He respects our freedom.

I remember a very fine Catholic writer, an old man, recounting how his common sense wife told him not to worry about his personal salvation as God had too much on his mind to be worried about one more individual! The writer replied by quoting what modern computers can do, the millions of pieces of information they can sort and classify as a hint, a glimpse of God's knowledge.

God calls each of us; few are called to be monks, priests or religious. God calls us in our everyday lives, through our families, through our work to follow him. These ordinary problems and events around us are not obstacles, but the means to Christ and to holiness. Each and everyone has a vocation.

May we have the light to see what is God's will and the wisdom and strength to act.

"Blessings and Curses"
6TH SUNDAY IN ORDINARY TIME
Jer 17:5-8; 1Cor 15:12, 16-20;
Gospel: Luke 6:17, 20-26.

We have today the more difficult version of the Beatitudes, the sermon on the plain, after Jesus has come down from the mountain. This is the more difficult version because it includes a number of woes or curses, not of murderers or rapists or drug traffickers, but of the rich, the well-fed, those laughing and those of whom everyone speaks well. The other version is found in chapter 5 of St. Matthew's gospel, where the sermon is given on the mountain. The thought in Matthew is much better organised and there are no curses, although the second half of that chapter is also very challenging, including, as it does in this chapter of Luke, a demand that we love our enemies.

Both versions of the Beatitudes, and especially today's, are among the most difficult sayings of Our Lord to understand. What do they mean today in the twenty-first century? How would they have been understood by his listeners? Is it a sin or a crime to be rich or well-fed, to enjoy a good laugh or to have a universally accepted good reputation? When I look back at my notes from earlier occasions when I have preached on this topic, they are probably the most unsatisfactory of all my attempts to explain the gospel.

In the gospel reading we hear that the poor, those who weep, those hated for Christ's name, those who are hungry, are blessed.

Sometime the word is translated as *happy* rather than *blessed*, but this is a profound mistake and a much less accurate translation of the Greek word *makarios*. It is difficult enough in the light of our faith to understand how the poor, the hungry, those in tears are blessed, but it strains our belief too far to claim all these, and the persecuted, are happy. It is possible for the poor to be happy; sometimes they are happier than those who have too much. But those in tears are not happy, except in very rare circumstances, such as the Irish mother complaining that the only time she saw her son happy was when he was miserable.

Jesus' message is not limited to the sermon on the plain or the sermon on the mount, but it is an important part of the total message of Jesus framed to try and provoke his followers to listen to him. This is different from their hearing what he was saying and allowing it to wash over them (something which happens frequently to us, especially when we have heard the readings many times. Our minds easily slide into neutral!)

Jesus is calling us to see our daily concerns, our difficulties and our achievements in a further and deeper light, to move through them to another dimension. They are a starting point for the heart of his message, about the love which should dominate the life of every Christian and which will take us into the next life.

It is impossible to make sense of the beatitudes without a conviction that the one true God loves us, especially in our misfortunes, and will reward those who suffer disproportionately from too much sickness, misfortune or violence and also reward those who are persecuted for following Christ.

Today one of the most telling differences between Christians and secularists, the new pagans, lies in their different attitudes to suffering.

Those without religion are more likely to ignore suffering or eliminate it through, e.g., abortion and euthanasia.

Christians are called to confront suffering, help those afflicted and believe that suffering can be made redemptive through faith and prayer.

Both the other readings are useful for understanding the meaning of the beatitudes. If Christ has not been raised from the dead, we will not rise either after death, and our sins have not been forgiven. If there is no after-life, the beatitudes are like a halftime speech to a football team everyone knows is bound to lose. As St. Paul wrote "If our hope in Christ has been for this life only, we are the most unfortunate of all people".

The first reading from the Old Testament prophet Jeremiah helps us understand what the woes, or curses, the "alas for you" mean. It is a warning to those who put all their trust in this life, the things of the flesh, and refuse both to trust in God and to be concerned with others, especially outsiders who are suffering. Those condemned are short-sighted, as well as selfish, tempted to believe that the things of the here and now are the sum total of reality. They are like dry scrub in the wasteland. We have to go beyond the surface of good public relations to the reality of God and love and forgiveness.

The beatitudes are worth our prayer and pondering, among Jesus' most beautiful teachings. They are a shot across our bows, a reminder not to become complacent, too pleased with ourselves, so that God and the unfortunate slip out of focus and perhaps off the screen. The beatitudes are like a suspension bridge between earth and heaven and constitute the language or currency of God's kingdom.

"Love Your Enemies"

7TH SUNDAY IN ORDINARY TIME

Samuel 26:2,7-9,12-13,22-23; 1 Corinthians 15:45-49;

Gospel: Luke 6:27-38.

I remember many years ago at junior secondary school being involved in a discussion on the consequences of removing one or two of the Commandments. My memories are muddled and we might also have discussed the advantages of having a holiday from one or more of the Commandments. Which one would we choose to retire temporarily, so that life would be easier and more attractive? Not surprisingly, we all quickly agreed on removing the sixth, because being young and naïve we all thought then that was the hardest Commandment to keep. The difficulty of the Commandments for each of us varies from person to person and indeed from time to time and a person might easily meet the standards in one area and have great difficulty in another. Some people always have trouble with the sixth Commandment.

Years later, when lecturing to future Catholic teachers, I explained that sexual sins, generally or regularly, are not the worst sins (although there is no doubt that they are serious sins; and when combined with violence, as in rape, or with young victims as in paederasty, they are very bad indeed). However, generally they are not the worst sins. One young university student objected vehemently that he had read somewhere that sexual sins were the worst sins and even got my permission to leave the class to search for the book where this was written. He returned and admitted that the book did not back his claim.

Our Lord understood human struggle and human weakness. While he did not encourage us to indulge our weakness, he did not condemn it as fiercely as he condemned hypocrisy or the injustice of the rich. While he did not condemn the woman accused of adultery; neither did he say to her, "You are doing well. Keep up the good work!" He said simply, "Go and sin no more." (John 8:11)

Now with the benefit of some years of experience, I believe that the Gospel passage of today contains some of Our Lord's most beautiful and most difficult moral teaching, i.e., the obligation to forgive our enemies, to pray for them and to do good to them. We are called to forgive those who hurt us and, probably more difficult still, to forgive those who hurt the ones we love.

Sometimes that requires a triumph of grace, the overcoming of every human instinct for hatred and revenge. It needs humility and sometimes it needs a long period of time.

I was deeply moved in late 2000 by the surviving father of some atrocity in Northern Ireland, who had lost members of his family through murder. He asked publicly on T.V. that no one take revenge for that terrible crime, because it would only mean another family grieving like himself over more deaths. He knew that if we continue to take an eye for an eye, then everyone will finish blind.

At ordinary times we Christians can accept the goodness and usefulness of forgiveness. The crunch comes when extreme situations strike us.

It is not for nothing that Our Lord taught us to pray in the "Our Father" that we should not be led into temptation. We should pray that we are not put to the test in extreme situations, because not one of us can predict with absolute certainty how we would react.

I remember reading Anthony Beevor's book on the battle for Stalingrad in the Second World War between the Germans and Russians. Millions of soldiers and civilians were killed and captured on the Eastern Front. It is a story of incredible bravery, remarkable heroism and shocking cruelty; often by the same people. It was kill or be killed in the grossest circumstances. Suffering on both sides bred an implacable hate.

There have also been a number of T.V. shows on the Russian front, the largest battles in history, including interviews with survivors of both sides from the World War against the Nazis. One survivor of the Warsaw ghetto, which was obliterated, said of his hatred for the Nazis, "If you could lick my heart it would poison you." So again I say, let us pray that we not be put to the test.

One common reaction on the need to forgive is to claim that while Our Lord's teaching is a good thing, we could not be expected to follow it in this particular set of circumstances; the offence is too great, we are not super-human and we feel these things too deeply.

Sometimes then a useful start is to pray for those who have upset us, even though we fear the prayer might choke us. And then often, slowly, our feelings follow our decision to pray and so continue the process of forgiveness.

Of course, we have to meet the minimum standard for good pagans – love those who love us, do good to those who do good to us. Sometimes, perhaps often, especially with those closest to us, we do not even meet those standards.

Over the centuries theologians and philosophers have speculated on the levels of altruism, which are necessary or practical.

We have already mentioned the Iron rule of a tooth for a tooth, but we know of other variants short of the Golden rule that we do to others what we would want them to do to us.

The Tinsel rule, favoured by short-sighted and un-Christian commonsense urges us to treat others as they deserve to be treated, while the Jewish teacher Hillel, a contemporary of Jesus, taught the Silver rule that we should not do to others what we ourselves hate.

These are far short of the profound and demanding teachings of Our Lord found here in chapter six of Luke's gospel.

The Gospel passage concludes by reminding us that we are called to be compassionate; to oppose evil resolutely. Sometimes to call a spade a spade, without judging the human heart. That is God's business and human motivation is often a mystery, even to the agents themselves.

Then Our Lord concludes with a promise and a warning. Give — and you will receive gifts. Forgive — and you will be forgiven, because the amount we measure out is the amount we will be given back.

"The Blind should not lead the Blind"

8TH SUNDAY IN ORDINARY TIME
Ecc 27:4-7; 1 Cor 15:54-58;
Gospel: Luke 6:39-45.

The warning against the blind leading the blind has passed into the English language as a judgement on incompetent leadership. The condemnation of hypocrisy, of seizing on the small faults of others while we ignore our more grievous personal defects is also well known in Christian circles, even if the warning is sometimes ignored in public life.

In chapter six Luke has gathered together a disparate group of Our Lord's teachings introduced after his appointment of the apostles. The Beatitudes, the commandment to love our enemies, the injunction not to judge others immediately precede the warning about the blind man leading others into a pit and the claim that the good tree produces good fruit.

Good intentions by themselves are never a guarantee in any sphere of life that we are heading in the correct direction, that we are not riding for a fall. Appealing to someone's good intentions as a justification is like someone claiming he has followed his conscience. We presuppose that good intentions and a proper conscience are necessary for integrity. It is a further question whether the good will and the moral judgements are adequate and correct, or mistaken.

We know that Jesus was severely critical of some of the religious leaders and teachers of his day and he was warning against them in these paragraphs.

It is not a controversial claim to point out that a disciple will always be like his teacher, although the general claim that "a disciple is not superior to his teacher" seems to need clarification, because all good teachers would hope that at least some, perhaps all, of their disciples or students would be better than themselves.

Our Lord is insisting that everyone should be open to new learning and he is condemning the arrogance and lack of humility that lead a pupil to look down on his teacher and be ungrateful for what he has received.

The Old Testament book of Leviticus (19:17) legislates for fraternal correction, insisting that he who administers the correction must be aware of his own faults, great or small. The word "hypocrite" is the Greek term for an actor and we have to look behind the actor's masks. All this now constitutes a good part of what we might call "Christian common sense".

Often today we will claim that a good tree produces good fruit and we are disconcerted when a bad tree seems to produce good fruit or a good tree produces bad fruit.

Jesus was not announcing a mathematical and universal principle but a general rule of thumb which is regularly true, especially when we have correctly judged the tree. Sometimes trees appear to be healthier than they are in reality.

Even today the heart is still the symbol for the source of love and goodness. A sincere person is described as "speaking from his heart" and just as we cannot pick figs from thorns or grapes from brambles so a good person should not regularly speak unkindly or untruths or even nonsense.

The excerpt in the first reading from the Book of Ecclesiasticus probably lies behind Our Lord's observations. Today we say that the proof of the pudding is in the eating. In those days they appealed to the pot to judge the quality of the potter and to a sieve to identify the rubbish.

Ecclesiasticus is quite clear that the test of any person lies in his speech. We should not praise anyone before he has spoken. Speech is the test because it comes from our hearts, whether they be dry and cold or warm and loving. Probably our hearts, not our minds are wise or foolish.

Jesus is right in his claim that a person's words flow out of what fills the heart, for good or ill. Heart speaks to heart.

"Christ Tempted Also"
1ST SUNDAY OF LENT
Deut 26:4-10; Rom 10:8-13;
Gospel: Luke 4:1-13.

Today is the First Sunday of Lent, when we begin our period of preparation for the most important Christian feasts at Easter and in this season we should be about our major spring cleaning (although it is autumn), where we have the annual overhaul not just of our morals but also of our faith. Is this likely to happen?

In our media dominated society the Christian rhythm of the seasons is regularly pushed to one side, although we do have public holidays at Christmas and Easter. Santa Claus and the Easter Bunny are promoted more than Christ and we have to work harder to find the proper emphasis in our preparations, or even to remember that we should be practising some penances and fasting from meat on Fridays of Lent. Every one of us here who has reached the age of reason (7) should have committed themselves to some penitential practices.

While the gospel is about the temptations of Christ in the wilderness the first two readings remind us of the importance of faith and of the great things God has done for us his people. Paul tells us: "By believing from the heart you are made righteous; by confessing with your lips you are saved."

The refrain of the psalm runs in a similar direction as we prayed "Be with me, Lord, when I am in trouble", while the verses sing

God's praises, who protects those "who dwell in the shadow of the Most High and abide in the shade of the Almighty".

Faith and morals are generally linked together closely in the lives of Christians, because the livelier our faith the more we shall struggle to lead good lives, follow the commandments and be generous and open to others.

All of this leads me to suggest that we examine the quality of our faith in the one true God and Jesus Christ his only Son at this time of Lent. Faith changes as we grow up, receive more and more education, face life's challenges and mature, but this need not mean that our faith becomes weaker. For saints it becomes not only stronger, but more simple, radical in its fruitfulness. For most of us, please God, our faith should become more rooted in our hearts as we grow old and overcome our doubts, hesitations and difficulties, so that our faith becomes leaner and tougher, but also richer.

We cannot click our fingers to make our faith stronger and many saints have endured periods of blackness when the consolations of faith were absent. The Little Flower, St. Therese of Lisieux, went through such a dark night. I once quizzed a priest friend of mine on his devotion to the Little Flower saying that I was surprised by his enthusiasm. His reply surprised me, because he explained that it was precisely her struggle with doubt and despair which inspired him.

We all know that a good life helps our faith, and on the other hand regular sin often produces moral and spiritual blindness. Faith is best nourished by regular prayer and some sort of religious reading; ideally a slow meditative reading of the scriptures (perhaps a small or longer passage every day), but any sort of good religious reading. We need to be nourished by God's word, directly or indirectly, because if we never pray or read religiously outside Sunday Mass, this must increase the spiritual and psychological pressures against our personal faith.

Every priest is required to pray the prayer of the Church each day for himself and his people. I am sure that this obligation also recognises the need of every baptised Christian including the priest, for spiritual nourishment. A crop needs good rains if there is going to be any fruit for harvesting.

When Satan tempted Jesus to turn stones into bread, Our Lord refused telling him that "Scripture says: Man does not live on bread alone."

This quotation is from chapter 8 of the Old Testament book of Deuteronomy, where the Jewish people on their Exodus journey from Egypt were locked in the desert, far from the Promised Land, sighing for the fleshpots of Egypt and whingeing about Moses and Aaron. Despite this betrayal, God still fed them with manna, dew and quails.

While Israel stumbled, Our Lord made no such mistake and rejected Satan's idolatrous suggestion and temptation to make prosperity a first priority. Because God comes first, even social justice work cannot be first, although it is a high priority Christian duty.

We do not need to travel to any metaphorical Egypt to try and find fulfilment in materialism and pleasure; in other words through self-seeking, selfishness. We need to remind ourselves that we too cannot live on bread alone and that a good Lent of extra prayer and some extra penances should strengthen our faith and also tone us up, make us better equipped to struggle against our fat relentless egos and for goodness in our society.

Satan then tempts Jesus with the power and glory of earthly kingdoms. Because Jesus' kingdom is not of this world, he refused.

Political activity in a democracy can help to preserve and extend the good society. But such power is not at the heart of Christian life and the abuse of power is a regular temptation for some, both in less important matters and in hugely important areas. How many lives have been lost in unjustified wars, grabs for more and more power.

The final temptation entices Jesus to abandon prudence, to place himself in God's hands and ask for an unnecessary miracle by throwing himself off the parapet of the Jerusalem Temple. Once again the Lord rejects this call to a supernatural extravaganza, rebuking the devil for putting the Lord-God to the test.

We should not be surprised when we are tempted and should always remember that it is not sinful to be tempted. We should follow Jesus' lead and reject temptation.

"Why Transfigured?"

2ND SUNDAY OF LENT

Gen 15:5-12, 17-18; Phil 3:17-4:1;
Gospel: Luke 9:28-36.

As we commence the second week of Lent, we continue our time of preparation for the great feast of Easter.

The first reading about Abraham and the one true God, reminds us that we are part of a long, almost 4000 year old, tradition. To realise we are part of God's people and plan should help us to improve in our struggle to do as we should at Lent. We are called to "seek the face of God who is our light and salvation".

In the second reading St. Paul bluntly rejects those who make their first priority money, food, and pleasure. He also promises the resurrection of our miserable bodies in the next life. When God is our light, we see more clearly and identify more accurately. Suffering and defeats are not the end of our story, or the end of the Christian story.

In today's gospel we have Luke's account of the transfiguration. For many years I was baffled about the reasons why the Church assigned this reading to this Sunday in Lent. But I now think it is placed here to emphasis the importance of strong faith, of being clear about priorities. The miracle of the transfiguration is recounted in all the synoptic gospels, and Luke seems to follow Mark's account. There are however a number of differences between the two versions, and Luke's account has perhaps 15 to 20 similarities with the account provided in Matthew's gospel.

In the transfiguration, the three key disciples – Peter, James and John – are taken to Mount Tabor by Jesus so that they can "see" the Kingdom of heaven in its glory. The transfiguration is closely connected with Jesus' baptism, which began his ministry in Galilee, with Jesus coming under the power of the Holy Spirit and being identified as the Son of the Father. This is immediately preceded in Luke's gospel by Jesus foretelling his passion to the disciples.

The transfiguration is not a messianic enthronement, because Jesus is more than a Messiah. He is not another Moses or Elijah, but God's Son and Chosen One, despite the suffering and death that he must undergo.

The glimpse here of Jesus' glory is also connected with his risen state, because the end of Our Lord's life will not simply be a repudiation of suffering and death. The miracle of the transfiguration occurred after this discourse on discipleship and his prediction of his suffering, death, and resurrection.

In the transfiguration, the trio of Moses, Elijah and Jesus talked about Jesus' "exodus", his progress to the promised land, and his glory. So once again we have the categories of Jewish salvation history to explain Jesus' role. However it is difficult to relate Elijah to the Jewish escape from Egypt (despite his journey to Mount Horeb). This raises the question of why Moses and Elijah were present at the transfiguration, rather than other figures. This is probably because they represent respectively the law and prophets of the Old Testament, and confirm the muddled Jewish expectation (around the time of Jesus' birth) of the appearance on earth of Moses and Elijah.

The preeminence of Moses the lawgiver is evident in the Old Testament times, but it is not so clear why Elijah was chosen above the other major prophets. After all he left no written texts.

We know that he was expected as a precursor to the Messiah, but I believe he had a unique role in the defence of monotheism when it was threatened with extinction by Ahab and the even more notorious Jezebel. Elijah should be our patron as we struggle against rising unbelief.

Moses and Elijah represent the old dispensation, and so they disappear in the miracle, leaving only Jesus.

The cloud that descends is a traditional symbol of the presence of God, as it was over the tabernacle in the desert.

For the sake of Peter, James and John, Jesus is described as "my Son" and "my Chosen One", just as Israel was called by the Lord "my chosen one". These titles confirm that Jesus is the messiah.

What was the transfiguration? For some it is just a visionary experience like that experienced by many saints and mystics. Some scholars suggest that it was in fact a post-resurrection appearance, which the three synoptics gospels transposed into an earlier setting. Some even argue that it was an invented appearance to symbolise Jesus' unique importance in salvation history.

Obviously the Catholic answer is that the transfiguration was an historical event in Jesus' Galilean ministry, which occurred not long after Peter's profession of faith in him as the Son of God.

It is not a conclusive argument against the historicity of the transfiguration that Peter later denied Christ, because when Peter did this he was scared, wanting only to escape. Hence his guilt about his betrayal and his cowardice. Without the transfiguration Peter would have been even weaker.

The transfiguration vividly recalls us to the mystery of God's love for us. We should take time to dwell on this and to pray about it. The thirteenth century English bishop and saint, Richard of Chichester once wrote in words that have since become famous:

O holy Jesu, most merciful Redeemer, friend and brother
May I know you more clearly, love you more dearly,
and follow you more nearly, day by day.

May this be our prayer this Lent and may it inform our Lenten preparations.

"St. Patrick and Enduring Faith"
3RD SUNDAY OF LENT
Ex 3:1-8, 13-15; 1 Cor 10:1-6, 10-12;
Gospel: Luke 13:1-9.

It is a good thing to celebrate the feast of Saint Patrick for a whole variety of reasons. I want to mention briefly two of these reasons this morning and the first is to remind ourselves of the tradition to which we belong and secondly to publicly express our gratitude to all those who have gone before us in this country, but especially to the Irish Australians who brought the faith to this land and who, not exclusively, but primarily, planted the faith in this great continent. And also St. Patrick's Day is a welcome diversion from the practice of Lent!

Lent is certainly about doing penance, being good and repenting in preparation for Easter. But just as the following of Jesus' teaching cannot be reduced to doing good and avoiding evil, so too the period of Lent should be a time when we strive to purify and strengthen our faith. At times all of us, devoted churchgoers as we are, we too at times can find it hard to believe as strongly as we should. It might be a tragedy, it might be a great personal disappointment that unbalances us, almost unhinges us. Our faith can come under severe pressure, because personal faith is not an immutable personal possession, like a wallet in our pocket, but a conviction of heart and mind. It is an enduring decision to love and to believe.

We know that this is an ancient quest, which goes back a couple of thousand years before Patrick. In the first Reading we hear of Moses, the liberator and lawgiver, then a refugee from the Egypt of his childhood, encountering the one true God in the symbol of the burning bush, burning without being consumed. Moses is afraid there, struck by fear, and Moses is asked to practise reverence, to take off his shoes, because it is holy ground around the burning bush. God told Moses that he was the same God who was reverenced by the Jewish fathers; Abraham, our father in faith, and Isaac and Jacob. Moses covered his face, unable to look at God.

Some years ago I visited St. Catherine's Monastery on the Sinai peninsula, one of the oldest monasteries in the world (founded in 527 A.D.) where a richly green, succulent plant grows on the spot where the burning bush is supposed to have been. For some reason, I had imagined the burning bush as a dry, scrawny gum. The green was a surprise.

So on this St. Patrick's Day we could amend this claim with complete truth, to say that this God we are reverencing is the God of Abraham and Moses and the prophets, and is also the God of St. Patrick and St. Brigid, and of the Irish missionaries to Europe, such as Columbanus to France and Northern Italy, and Columba to Scotland, of St. Oliver Plunkett, who was the last Catholic martyr of the Reformation in England, and of our Irish ancestors, priests and lay people and religious, who planted the faith in this fair land of ours, who worked so valiantly and so well here and who built the magnificent Cathedrals in Melbourne and Sydney.

We Irish Australians and the Irish are not just united by blood. We are much less separated than in the past because of modern communications. But whether we are in Ireland or Australia or in the other outposts of the Irish Diaspora, we are united by our faith, our Christian monotheism, in the Catholic tradition.

When archbishop of Melbourne I arranged for a fine bronze statue of Archbishop Mannix, by the English sculptor Nigel Boonham to be erected in front of the Cathedral. I had proposed putting on a little explanatory plaque that Archbishop Mannix was Ireland's greatest gift to Australia and I gave that to a number of people for comment, including the Irish ambassador. One of the historians I sent it to said this was not true. Archbishop Mannix was not Ireland's greatest gift to Australia because the Catholic faith was Ireland's greatest gift and he was absolutely correct.

Returning to our Old Testament story, Moses asked the good God what else He had to say and God replied that he knew of his people's sufferings in Egypt and promised them a land flowing with milk and honey. He, God, means to deliver his people from the hands of the Egyptians.

Moses went further. "What is your name?" he asked God and received the strange reply, "I am Who I am". Books have been written on this and theologies constructed. God is not anything physical or material; is not a particular person, but a spiritual Force of Love and Intelligence; more, not less than a person. We now say that Almighty God is transcendent, i.e., much greater and beyond the forces of nature, which can sometimes be so cruel, perhaps particularly here in Australia; droughts, floods, and in other parts of the world, cyclones and earthquakes. Some Greens today turn nature into a type of god, but our God is the maker and sustainer of nature. God is not the god of scientific gaps, whom we use to explain what we cannot understand. God is beyond all the forces of the universe and history. God wrote the laws of nature, started the process of creation and history, keeps it going and will bring the whole process to a triumphant conclusion.

But the most useful piece of information we have about God is in the response to today's Psalm, "God is kind and merciful"; to everyone of us, young or old, Irish or Australian, man or woman, sinner as well as saint.

Our brother Jesus, Son of God and Son of Mary, brings God down to our level, makes God much more accessible to us. It is easier to love Jesus than to love the almighty, invisible, omnipotent Spirit of God.

It is a great mystery to try and work out how God acts through nature and through history. Why do bad things happen to good people? Why do bad people sometimes seem to prosper? If misfortune strikes us, is it because we have been evil, or perhaps our parents or grandparents were evil? Why did Our Lady and Our Lord suffer so much?

In today's Gospel, Our Lord explains that God does not work like this. The victims of Pilate, those people killed by his soldiers, had not deserved their fate, they were not sinners any more than the rest of us, just as the people who were killed when the tower at Siloam collapsed. Sometimes today we still need to tell people this, because the instinct of many of us can be to imagine that God is punishing us when we are hit by illness or some freak accident.

Christ then goes on and explains that when the call of God is answered or refused, consequences follow from that answer. Come follow me is a command as well as an invitation.

God does not punish genuine ignorance. But a knowing rejection of the invitation brings us into another category, like the fig tree which was producing no fruit.

I was once at a conference for young Catholic adults. My topic, a good topic for us all and especially for young people, was "The Need for Conversion" – a somewhat drab title as I discovered.

There were two brothers, both law students, giving talks. One was giving a talk on Heaven, which he entitled "An Uplifting Experience" and the other on Purgatory, which he entitled "Purgatory – A Burning Issue". Earlier the older brother had given a talk at his university on the Resurrection entitled "The Resurrection – The Original Rolling Stone". In an attempt to excite a little enthusiasm, I renamed my talk on Conversion, "Turn or Burn".

Sin is a reality and in faith we believe that the scales of justice do work out over eternity. Now the first and most important thing we must always remember is that the Lord is kind and merciful, but unrepentant sinners bring punishment on themselves. We must continue to choose God and goodness, to repent and do penance for our sins.

Let us pray this morning that the core of the Irish contribution to Australia, the Catholic faith will always remain strong here, because it is the faith that is at the centre of so much that has distinguished the Irish tradition. It is from the faith that the Irish Australians got their passion for justice, it was the faith that sustained them in the struggle to build good families and it was the faith that brought single men and women, priests and religious, from the other side of the world to a hostile and difficult environment to share that faith and goodness. Let us pray in gratitude for that, let us pray for the continued flourishing of the faith and let us pray that we shall use this Lent to renew our own faith as well as our heart, so that we can celebrate Easter with a greater faith and greater love.

"Our Loving Father and his Older Son"
4TH SUNDAY OF LENT
Ex 32: 7-11; 13-14; 1 Tim 1:12-17;
Gospel: Luke 15:1-3:11-32.

We all know that Our Lord was a wonderful teacher, having more influence than any other teacher in history, and that he was a marvellous storyteller. If we really want to understand what Our Lord is about, the best place to start is in his teachings and particularly with his parables because often they move in unexpected directions. They are unpredictable.

Today we have probably the best known story of Our Lord, the story of the Prodigal Son. However, it is not really a story about the prodigal son. It should have a different title because it is a story about God, about the nature of God, what God is like. It is the parable of the good father. A sub-title might be the parable of the two brothers.

The details of the story ring true if we are going to set it in Our Lord's time because the Jews then lived not just in Israel – as we call it today – Palestine, but throughout the Roman Empire and throughout the Middle East. It is estimated there were about four million through the Empire, that is ten percent of the total population, and there was half a million at home in Palestine. So the younger brother would have had tons of friends or family, cousins, aunts or uncles, and he would have gone to a Jewish community in some other place.

The older brother was very steady, worked at home with his father, a hard worker, had never given much trouble at all. The younger fellow was a different type altogether, as often happens in families. He said to his father, "Give me my share of the inheritance, I want to go off and make a lot of money and have a lot of fun." For some reason or other his father agreed, gave him the money equivalent to his share of the farm, and he headed off. Is it too much of a modern reading to conjecture that the father respected the free choice of his younger adult son?

There might have been an economic downturn, it might have been just that he could not handle money, was too extravagant with the riotous life that he led. At any rate, he lost everything. There were no social security provisions then and as you know pigs were unclean to the Jews. They do not touch pork, but the only job where he could get food to put in his mouth was to work with the pigs.

And it was there that the conversion process began. It was not terribly exalted or spiritual, at least initially, because he said to himself, "I could be home working for dad on one of the farms and I would be much better off than I am here looking after the pigs and having to eat their food", and it developed from there. He was able to say, "Yes, I have sinned before God and before my father", and so he started to head for home.

When the father saw his son, he ran out to greet him. They ate meat very rarely; he killed the prize calf so that they could have an enormous feast, a great welcome home party. Few people wore shoes, but he gave him sandals to show that his dignity had been restored. Fewer people wore a ring and he gave him his ring back to show that he had been restored as a son of the family. So all was marvellous, a very happy return.

Then, as in real life, something goes wrong. The older brother turns up and complains about his long absent younger brother who has squandered his part of the inheritance.

Once again the father was kind and conciliatory, explaining 'No, no. Everything I have is yours. The farm is going to be yours. I am deeply grateful for everything you have done, but this young fellow was lost and now he is found. He was dead and now he has come to life.'

It is well known that the older brothers in the Old Testament often do not do well or come off second best. We have the treachery of Cain towards Abel, the fortunes of Ishmael and Isaac, of Esau and Jacob and the eleven older brothers' mistreatment of their youngest brother Joseph, his father Jacob's favourite. These mishaps provide one reason, among many, why the Jewish people do not like to be called the older brothers of the Christians!

In this parable the older brother was certainly small minded and somewhat mean spirited, but he was genuinely offended by what he saw as the rewarding of an act of open rebellion. He was called to more than that, called to overcome the often unrecognised envy of those who are regularly faithful towards those who kick over the traces and then seem to be rewarded disproportionately when they see the light.

I sometimes quote the occasion when a group of senior-year secondary students at a wealthy boys' school shouted in chorus their support for the cause of the older brother! They were at least partly genuine but one or two of them might have been better advised to support the younger man!

For older people like myself who were brought up in a world where the Christian teaching was more severe, the story provides a nice balance, perhaps even a corrective, explaining what God is like. To the young people who have grown up in an entirely different Christian sort of ethos or world, it is also a good lesson because I am sure that the prodigal son is like many young people today. When things go really wrong the great temptation is to think that they are absolutely worthless, there is nowhere to turn, nobody to welcome them; it is not worth the battling and the striving. In other words, their self-image has been so destroyed by circumstances and their own mistakes that there is nowhere to go. And this story of the good father reminds them that no matter how many other humans might turn them down, God will always have them back and accept them.

This encouraging parable reminds us of the need for repentance, for individual Confession, for a personal celebration of the Sacrament of Penance. For us to follow the example of the Prodigal Son, it doesn't matter whether we are more like the older brother or whether we are more like the young fellow, as long as we are battling on, trying to do our best, however imperfectly. The Sacrament of Penance, of Reconciliation, is one of the most beautiful services that the Church offers to people. Sometimes it can be a little bit like going to the dentist. I don't think I have ever met anyone who really likes to go to Confession especially when they are carrying some heavier guilt, but so many people know and will testify how wonderfully healing and liberating the love and the forgiveness of God is, especially when received in the sacrament of forgiveness.

So let us make a resolution to go to Confession, to repent and celebrate the Sacrament of Reconciliation and let us try to plant deeper our heart this image of the God who loves us and always forgives us.

"The Entry into Jerusalem"

PALM SUNDAY (i)
Gospel: Luke 19:28-40

Holy Week is now beginning, those seven days of preparation for the Resurrection, during which we also remember the Last Supper (when we celebrate the ministerial priesthood), Christ's death and his time in the tomb before the Resurrection.

This week of celebrations probably dates from early fourth century Jerusalem, from that period when the Christians first obtained their freedom, so that they could publicly re-enact Our Lord's journey to Calvary (rather than celebrate in private and in secret).

In Luke's gospel Jesus' long journey is now over as he arrives into Jerusalem, the city of his destiny and visits the Temple, the house of his Father. There are similar accounts of this event, different in some respects, in all four gospels, John as well as the three synoptics.

Jesus comes to Jerusalem as a pilgrim, is hailed as a king with probably a percentage of the crowd, as well as all the later readers of the gospels, seeing him as the Messiah. Unexpectedly for the majority of onlookers, this small triumph will be followed quickly by a period of teaching, the disturbance in the Temple with the moneychangers and then by Jesus' passion and death. Our Lord will perform his own exodus, just as the Jews escaped from Egypt, and eventually Easter peace will be attained.

It was quite a small triumph as we shall see, but this success is not the reason why Jesus is remembered or celebrated, because it was not the cause or occasion of our salvation. It is not even like the first course in a fine dinner, because it takes us in the wrong direction of worldly success. It in fact is an anti-climax, a false lead.

Our instincts are like Peter's who was fiercely rebuked by Our Lord when he insisted that Jesus should not suffer and who used his sword in the garden of Gethsemane in attempting to resist Jesus' arrest. Jesus is going to suffer and die and our redemption is achieved by this.

The entry into Jerusalem is a small consolation before the saving catastrophe.

In my childhood, like all children, I suffered under a number of misapprehensions, misunderstood events that I now see more clearly. I thought that the entry into Jerusalem would have been like a football grand final or like a royal visit fifty years ago with tens of thousands of people participating.

There was only a smallish crowd, probably less than a thousand, many of them from up-country Galilee. We do not know how many women and children participated, but they were noisy, charismatic types and delighted to welcome Our Lord.

Luke does not mention the palm branches Matthew described as being laid down on the road but we do hear of their laying down their cloaks for his procession, in the way that we today would roll out the red carpet for the visit of a high official.

In a revealing detail Luke has the crowd shouting out "peace and glory in the heavens", whereas at the nativity the angels were proclaiming peace on earth. There was not going to be peace in Jerusalem for Jesus and his followers for some days yet.

Jesus' opponents urged him to stop this unseemly enthusiasm by the crowd, this exaggerated behaviour tending towards blasphemy, but he gave them no comfort. If they were silent, he replied, the stones themselves would cry out.

We have now entered Holy Week, the most solemn series of feasts in the Church's calendar. Let us be serious and prayerful as we follow Jesus on his way to death on Calvary and his glorious resurrection.

"The Start of Holy Week"

PALM SUNDAY (ii)
Is 50:4-7; Phil 2:6-11;
Gospel: Luke 22:14-23:56.

We have moved through Lent briskly, as usually happens when we are busy, and now on this Palm Sunday, a happier name than Passion Sunday, we are once again entering Holy Week.

We have a range of beautiful ceremonies before us: the Chrism Mass for the blessing of the sacramental oils when we priests renew our commitment to the promises made at ordination, the Mass of the Lord's Supper, the Good Friday ceremonies when no Mass is celebrated before the climax of the Easter Vigil and the Easter Sunday Masses. I urge you all to attend as many of the ceremonies as possible. Certainly no believing Catholic should miss coming to the Church on Good Friday. The Easter Vigil ceremonies constitute the centre-piece of the Christian year and while they might be a bit long, they are rich in wonderful symbolism. Holy Week therefore is a special period for extra prayer, as we express out thanks to Christ Our Lord for the fact that we have been redeemed. In other words God will forgive our sins when we repent, and we have the prospect of eternal life and happiness after death, despite our sins and indifferent performance.

In the first reading today the Old Testament prophet Isaiah acknowledged that he had to listen like a disciple and the Lord has opened his ears for that purpose.

As a celebrant and preacher, I pray that, like Isaiah, the Lord will give me a disciple's tongue. But that will be impossible if I do not have a disciple's ear to listen to the Word of God in the Scriptures and to recognise the many movements of the Spirit in the world around us; while also trying to identify where the spirit of evil is working to draw people away from the straight and narrow path which leads to salvation.

Jesus is not remembered for the happy event of his welcome into Jerusalem. It was good and appropriate that his disciples acknowledged Jesus for what he was, but the Palm Sunday procession was only a small, less important part of the process which won salvation for us.

Our Lord's enemies were plotting his death. He realised this and his apostles refused to believe the game was afoot and moving towards an undesired conclusion.

Holy Week reminds us that the struggle between good and evil continues in every generation, across every community and within every human heart!

That is why Lent is a particularly appropriate time to go to confession, to receive absolution in the Sacrament of Penance. When we are forgiven and healed and our conscience is clear, we are much better placed to enter the lists to struggle for God and goodness in the wider society.

Holy Week reminds us that we cannot dodge the issue. Everyone has to declare himself for or against God and goodness.

"Anointed"

CHRISM MASS OF HOLY WEEK
Is 61:1-3, 6, 8-9; Apoc 1:5-8;
Gospel: Luke 4:16-21

Holy Thursday is the day before we commemorate Jesus' death on a cross at Jerusalem nearly 2000 years ago. Today we remember in a special way Our Lord's celebration of the Last Supper, which we repeat in a certain real sense when we celebrate Mass, i.e., the Eucharist.

So I welcome in particular all those young Catholics present this morning for Mass and for the blessing of the oils, which are used at baptism and confirmation, for the ordination of priests and bishops and for the anointing of the sick.

Today is also a special feast for those of us who are priests, because Jesus ordained the apostles as priests during the Last Supper. He did not lay his hands on them as the bishop now does, because that came later in the New Testament times with Paul, but he commanded his apostles to continue to celebrate the Eucharist in his memory.

Catholic adults generally are grateful for all the good work done by their priests, but sometimes when we are young, we might not notice these good deeds. If you are tempted to take your priest for granted, today is your chance to remedy that by praying for your parish clergy and all priests and by greeting him when you meet him at school or around the parish.

I would now like to say a few words on this Holy Week feast especially for the priests; but everyone is invited to listen!

In 2007 Pope Benedict XVI published his post-synodal exhortation, *The Sacrament of Love*, i.e., the Eucharist, which followed his first encyclical, *God is Love*. The Holy Father is right to emphasise the centrality of love in the Christian understanding of life. The first two commandments are the great commandments to love God and to love one another, while in the Eucharist we commemorate Divine love in action i.e. Jesus' suffering, death and glorious resurrection.

God himself is love "a perfect communion of love between Father, Son and Holy Spirit" so that in the Eucharist Jesus does not give us something, but Himself through his body and blood; so that we his followers become ever more truly the Body of Christ.

It is not a coincidence that the phrase "Body of Christ", following St. Paul again, is used for both the Eucharistic body, under the form of bread and wine and the community of Catholic believers. As the Holy Father remarks Christ and his Church are inseparable.

In the 1990s a few people spoke more frequently of the "official" church, often contrasting it with the "local" church community or the "real" church of parish believers or some other community. This was a bad category mistake, because there is only one Church, primarily and substantially existing in the Catholic community.

There are officials within the Church such as priests, bishops, nuns and brothers and the pope, just as there are many different institutions or communities, such as parishes, schools, hospitals, service agencies within the one true Church, but the Spirit sent by Christ works first of all from within the communitarian framework instituted by Christ himself. The Church is a mystery of communion founded on and nourished by the Eucharist. There is only one Church.

This is why the Church twice uses that beautiful passage from Isaiah in the readings for this Mass because it is through the official anointings of the sacraments of baptism, confirmation and holy orders that all Christians, and especially priests are called to give new sight to those who are muddled or confused (or blinded by the bright lights of the world), to bring freedom to those enslaved by evil habits, to preach the good news of salvation, not just to the clever, but to the poor and unlearned and to free those who are oppressed or imprisoned.

In the gospel we have Jesus in his home town synagogue of Nazareth reading the passage from Isaiah, although Luke's version is more like a paraphrase of Isaiah's message than the exact Old Testament text as we now have it.

Today the Christians of Nazareth have reconstructed the village as they believe it would have been in Jesus' time. To my surprise the synagogue was very small, holding only about 20 to 30 people. Perhaps there were many others outside.

As priests we need to remind ourselves in faith, despite the vivid awareness of our personal sins and deficiencies, that the Spirit which comes to us in all the sacraments, and especially the Eucharist, still empowers us and our people to produce growth in the Spirit, to provide healing and forgiveness, to nourish genuine human development just as it did in the time of Isaiah (and even more so) in Jesus' own time.

God is with us and the Spirit is in our hearts as we continue the vital work of the people of God in the challenging times through which we are passing.

In conclusion I ask that the one true God will bless our priestly efforts during this Holy Week to bring Christ to others. This is the goal of all Christian mission.

In Pope Benedict's first sermon in St. Peter's Square he said: "There is nothing more beautiful than to be surprised by the Gospel, by the encounter with Christ. There is nothing more beautiful than to know him and to speak to others of our friendship with him".

May we remember these words as we celebrate this Easter season.

"Empty Tomb"
EASTER NIGHT MASS
Rom 6:3-11;
Gospel: Luke 24:1-12

The Easter Vigil and the Easter Sunday Masses focus attention on the centre of our Catholicism: the claims of the risen Lord, Jesus the Crucified Christ, the only Son of the God of Abraham, Isaac and Jacob; the one true God, the good God.

The world around us is often religiously ignorant and even more frequently it is religiously confused. And we can be infected by these confusions, being tempted to see any religious enthusiasm as equally praise-worthy, because every religious faith is pretty similar.

It is always useful when judging religious claims to see how many times God and Christ are mentioned, whether their role is regarded as vital and central or whether they are tagged on as a mandatory refrain at the end. Catholic liturgies, indeed any recognisable Christian liturgy, is not about the celebration of community spirit, but must be God-centred acts of worship.

I once heard of some self-professed Catholics who claimed that God does not need people praying to Him. This would be characteristic of a tribal God, they claimed, whereas their notion of god was more sophisticated and drew upon the Upanishads, a Hindu holy book. The only God we worship is the Father of Jesus Christ, Our Lord and God, our crucified Lord. To reject this is idolatry and Jesus taught us in his special prayer, which we know as the Our Father, to pray to God regularly and even to pray for our daily bread.

Others will claim to be Catholic and deny the divinity of Christ. One might claim to be Christian in an attenuated sense by recognising only a human "lordship" in Christ, but one cannot claim to be Catholic and not believe in the divinity of Christ.

We can also find some others who would never dream of denying the one true God, never dream of denying the divinity of Christ His Son, but act as though the most important and central elements of Catholicism are not really matters of faith or meaning, but issues of morality. For some, what is really important is social justice; for others it is how we treat one another in our daily life, how we treat our family, friends, work mates.

Right and wrong, repentance and forgiveness are vital and necessary elements of following Christ as today's epistle makes very clear. Paul tells us our sinful bodies are to be crucified with Christ "to free us from the slavery of sin"; but knowing and believing in God is as important as morality. To follow Christ we need both.

The media also regularly lead us away from the central religious message of Easter (and Christmas) by fastening on some controversial or political aspect. Once at Easter time I gave a TV interview and received an unlisted question about the Holy Father's attitude to AIDS in Africa and how to deal with the epidemic. Predictably the ensuing controversy overshadowed the Easter message, although it did provide a good teaching opportunity; and in one TV poll scepticism about the overall effectiveness of condoms in the AIDS struggle received 49% support after being well ahead for most of the voting.

Many elements in the commentariat are regularly tempted to downplay or sideline the crucial role of Christianity in providing meaning, strength and consolation in the lives of most Australians, but often these critics only mix with one another.

The one true God is not a remote mysterious impersonal force, which manifests itself in all things, especially humans. Our God is personal, capable of loving us, of separating good from evil, of punishing and rewarding, not capriciously but by judging each person's heart of hearts.

Jesus is the Son of God and He explained that even in his risen state he is not a ghost, because ghosts have no flesh and bones. Mary Magdalene and Peter both found his body gone. His disciples could touch his hands; place a hand in his side as Thomas did. He also ate a piece of grilled fish. The Son of God demonstrates for us that our God is personal and loving; the greatest of all mysteries, but interested in us, not some upmarket supernatural force like gravity or electricity.

The good God inserted himself in history especially through his special pact with the Jewish people to whom Mary, Joseph and Jesus belonged and through his apostles and disciples. Our Lord is a product of this remarkable story of fidelity and sin, of prophecy and idolatry. In today's gospel we hear the first reports of the resurrection, of the women who were terrified by the absent body. Their reports were not believed and dismissed as nonsense. When Peter ran to the tomb and discovered these reports were true, he was amazed.

Later when Our Lord appeared, his followers were still alarmed and frightened. "Peace be with you" he said, the greeting each bishop repeats at the start of Mass. Peace is mentioned a number of times at Mass and just before Communion we exchange a sign of peace. Loving God requires us to keep the commandments, but if we believe and we strive to love unselfishly we will have more peace in our hearts. Easter insists that personal faith in a personal God is vital and this faith helps us to be good and to find peace.

"New Sight at Emmaus"

3RD SUNDAY OF EASTER – (YEAR A)
Acts 2:14, 22-33; 1 Ptr 1:17-21;
Gospel: Luke 24:13-35.

Naturally the Church continues to hammer home during this Easter Season the fundamental lessons of the Resurrection; Christ Our Lord's triumph through his life, suffering and death.

St. Peter too, many years later in his first letter emphasised again the value of our central Christian claims. We are saved, "paid for" or "ransomed" were the terms he chose, not by anything corruptible, not by silver or gold, but by the precious blood of the sacrificial lamb, Jesus himself.

Our Lord came from the Jewish tradition of monotheism and he always acknowledged the special pact or covenant between the one true God and his chosen people the Jews.

So it is not surprising that we hear in Luke's Acts of the Apostles how Peter explained the significance of Jesus' life and teaching through the Old Testament.

Peter explained that King David's prophecies about his successor apply to Jesus himself. David died and was buried. Peter noted that King David's tomb still existed then. Later it was lost for centuries and there is a site claimed for it today, without overwhelming evidence to support it I am told.

But Peter explained that there was no claim that David rose from the dead. Only Jesus did that. Here is the great difference between the religious strivings of good people, on the one hand, and God's unique series of interventions on the other.

The evidence is not clear in the way that a simple mathematical principle is clear. To understand and accept the Resurrection requires some effort, fundamental good will and a willingness to say "yes"; to commit oneself to follow. Following Christ is not simply intellectual and the basic propositions requiring our acceptance are not like fiercely difficult mathematical theorems, which might be demonstrably true, but are only open to those with high intelligence and years of training. We do need to be pure of heart to believe, "to see God" through the eyes of faith, but we do not need a university degree in order to believe. In our societies where an increasing minority are slaves to money and possessions, to disordered sexual practices and where Australia has about 90,000 abortions a year, it is not surprising that many find it hard to believe in God.

Today's gospel about the journey to Emmaus is a special favourite of artists and writers because it exemplifies the honest struggle, the good will and the human capacity to be blind to the truth, which everyone of us shares. It is one more example of how the first Christians coped with the claim that Jesus the Nazarene, the preacher from the country who was crucified, had risen from the dead.

Let us try to imagine the scene. Many of the disciples would have been in a state of shock still; their secret ambitions destroyed, because Christ was gone. They probably thought that all the time they had passed with Christ had been wasted. They were hurt no doubt by the jibes of their opponents.

Then just when they were settling down into the new situation, the women went and upset everything. There is probably some significance in the fact that women first discovered the Resurrection. They went, because women did the embalming – and perhaps because they had not given up hope.

These two disciples at Emmaus were not on the inner circle of Christ's followers; perhaps they hoped for the political liberation of Israel, "the one to set Israel free". They were certainly very confused when this stranger turned up and began to explain the scriptures to them.

Jesus explained how all the Old Testament prophets were a preparation for his method of dealing with evil; and it is useful to remember that they recognised Christ for what He was only after they had invited him to share their hospitality, a cup of tea and a light meal.

They practised simple everyday kindness and were rewarded for it. We remember Jesus' words on the Last Day and chapter 25 of Matthew's gospel on the separation of the saved from the damned through the presence or absence of simple acts of kindness alone. Sometimes we think this is an easier test than other Christian requirements but it is not always so, as we have to help not only those we love or like, but all people, even enemies, ingrates and frauds.

The Emmaus encounter should sensitise us to others, because after kindness and after Christ's breaking of the bread they recognised Jesus. So may it be with us.

"Physical Resurrection?"

3RD SUNDAY OF EASTER – (YEAR B)
Acts 3:13-15, 17-19; 1 Jn 2:1-5;
Gospel: Luke 24:35-48.

On one occasion at lunch in Cathedral House, Sydney, we priests were discussing what we might preach about for the third Sunday of Easter. I confessed that I was having some difficulty with the readings, which of course emphasise the reality of the risen Christ in his post-Resurrection appearances to the disciples.

It was not that we were lacking in appreciation of the importance of Christ Our Lord's resurrection, or embarrassed by it in any way. It is just that it can be difficult to preach on the Resurrection, especially to the same congregation and avoid repeating what we said for the last two weeks.

Probably even this is a mistaken calculation because most people are more likely to remember something when it is repeated, but some variety and a spread of teaching from a preacher are vital over the liturgical year.

I am a regular reader of an English weekly called *The Spectator* – always wonderfully written, often interesting, generally very secular, but with quite a few Christian, mostly Catholic writers.

In 2006 *The Spectator* asked 28 English public figures whether they believed "that Jesus physically rose from the dead".

The then Prime Minister Tony Blair, not yet a Catholic, but someone who attended Sunday Mass each week with his Catholic wife, declined to answer. An assistant for the Archbishop of Canterbury said he was very busy, would not be able to give a quote, but wanted to be put firmly in the "yes camp".

Cardinal Murphy O'Connor, the Catholic Archbishop of Westminster quoted St. Paul, "If Christ has not been raised, your faith is futile" (1 Cor 15:17) and explained that as a bishop at Easter "he proclaimed this truth on behalf of the believing community".

Richard Dawkins an atheist, then professor at Oxford University, conceded St. Paul's logic, but said the unpleasant truth is that our religion is null and void. "Nature does not owe us a meaningful life", he explained. "It is up to us to make it so". He did not explain the why and the how.

I was pleasantly surprised because most respondents believed in Our Lord's bodily resurrection and in the empty tomb, although they acknowledged the special status of this belief in faith, the absence of scientific evidence and, in some cases, they acknowledged too their doubts and weak faith. In other words they were believers, struggling to embrace the truth, just like us.

Today's gospel reminds us the first disciples needed a lot of convincing that the Lord had risen. They still did not believe as they discussed the Emmaus story and when Jesus did appear, they fell into a state of alarm and fear and thought they were seeing a ghost. It is not Catholic teaching that Our Lord's risen Body was physical in exactly the same way as we are. He arrived through closed doors, but he himself emphasised his bodily-ness as he asked the disciples to touch him and he took grilled fish from them and ate it. The Resurrection does not mean that Jesus' soul went marching on, while his body lay mouldering in the grave; nor can it be reduced to the simple survival of his memory among his family and followers.

Our faith insists that the God of Abraham, Isaac and Jacob glorified his Son Jesus Christ after his suffering and death and Jesus explained to his disciples how passages in the Law of Moses, the psalms and the prophets (from what we call the Old Testament) prophesied his suffering, death and resurrection and the remarkable fact that it would be announced to all nations that sins can be forgiven whenever there is repentance. This is one of the supreme fruits of the redemption.

A couple of other *Spectator* writers had interesting and particular insight on aspects of the Resurrection.

The first of these, Frank Johnson, had spent most of his life as a political journalist and therefore he claims that at each Easter he feels especially qualified to refute the theory that the apostles faked the resurrection, i.e., stole the body, paid the guards to be silent and stuck to their lies under persecution for the rest of their lives.

He says quite bluntly that no conspiracy to keep silent ever lasts. Someone talks. Most crimes are not solved by police breakthroughs, but by someone talking. He pointed out that it is very difficult to die for the truth and that the disciples would have been constrained to lie for years despite imprisonment and torture.

Even the Watergate conspiracy in 1972-3 to protect President Nixon of the United States, then the most powerful man in the world, started to unravel after a fortnight. Someone talked. On top of this it is clear that many of the disciples started out as cowards.

Matthew Paris is another *Spectator* writer, an atheist, who was surprised that most of the respondents to the survey did not duck or fudge the extraordinary claim to believe in Christ's resurrection. He too does not believe that the disciples made up any story, simply claiming that all the great religions Jews, Christians, Moslems, labour under gigantic misapprehensions.

We have heard all this before, but what is interesting is Paris' claim that Jesus must have existed and much of his teaching must have come down to us accurately because so much of what we Christians actually do is "the opposite of everything he (Jesus) was so plainly trying to teach". He says that Jesus is "the fly in the Church's ointment" and that is one reason why he, an avowed atheist, feels such huge respect for Our Lord.

The examples he gives trying to prove this point make up a mixed bag and it is no argument against Christ that we his followers do not live up to his high standards. But Paris is right: "If Jesus had been a hoax, the Church could have invented somebody so much more convenient."

Christ has died. Christ is risen. Christ will come again. We profess this faith with all the consolations and challenges that come in the package.

"Priests and Leaders Needed"

7TH SUNDAY OF EASTER – ASCENSION DAY
Acts 1:1-11; Eph 1:17-23;
Gospel: Luke 24:46-53.

Today is Ascension Day, when we celebrate Our Lord's final post-resurrection appearance and his departure for heaven. We used to celebrate this feast on Ascension Thursday, but with the demise of most holy days of obligation (a major feast, not on a Sunday, when in the past we were obliged to go to Mass), we now celebrate on the Sunday.

Tonight we have four young men from the Good Shepherd Seminary, in Sydney, who are formally being admitted as candidates for the priesthood in the Archdiocese of Sydney. We thank God for their generosity, for the care and supervision of the rector and seminary staff, as these seminarians progress towards priesthood.

This ceremony fits in nicely with the small excerpt from the first reading from the Acts of the Apostles, chosen by the Vatican authorities as the signature piece of Scripture for the World Youth Day, Sydney in 2008: "You will receive power when the Holy Spirit comes upon you, and then you will by my witnesses, not only in Jerusalem, but ... indeed to the ends of the earth."

These young men have answered a call to become priests and therefore servants of the people and witnesses to Christ's message and the Catholic tradition. We need them and many more, as well as young women, to step forward for leadership.

The logic of the situation is clear and it should be clear to all our young people who know Christ and love the Church. Unless young men and women step forward to serve and provide leadership, the vitality of the Church will diminish steadily. We thank God that men and women such as these candidates are answering Christ's call.

Jesus calls some people in every generation, including our own. The danger is that we cannot hear, because there is too much static or interference on the line, or because we refuse to tune into His wavelength.

In today's readings, we have two accounts of the Ascension, both written by Luke, with one taken from the conclusion of his gospel and the other from the beginning of the Acts of the Apostles, which tell the story of the early Church after Christ's resurrection.

Naturally both accounts agree on the essentials of the story. Some have objected to the notion of Jesus disappearing into the sky, but it would have been incongruous for the Lord to return to the earth. We now know that it is difficult to speak of "up" and "down" when talking about space. When I was a young priest in England the school kids would ask me why Australians do not fall off the planet as we live "down under"! Generally we speak of heaven in the sky and hell in the underworld.

The afterlife is a mystery, but Christ's bodily departure reminds us that we believe in the resurrection of the body as well as the final judgement on the last day.

The Greek philosopher Plato believed that the human intellect or soul was eternally related to the eternal principles of reason. This implied some sort of pre-existence and the survival of the individual soul after death. Christians believe, on Christ's word, that in the new heaven and earth we shall be in some real sense embodied spirits. At the ascension Christ foreshadowed this, by returning to heaven body and soul.

Christ has gone ahead in victory not just as one more outstanding member of the Church triumphant, but as the Son who sits at God's right hand, above every Sovereignty, Authority, Power and Domination (apparently different ranks of angels). He is the ruler of everything, the head of the Church which is His body and all things are under His feet. This is the same Christ who suffered, died and rose again.

When Paul wrote to the Christian community in Ephesus, a Roman Empire city where many buildings and the amphitheatre still survive, he urged God the father of glory to grant a spirit of wisdom and perception to them, so that the eyes of their minds might see the rich glories promised the saints and the wonderful nature of the hope towards which they are called.

May we all understand this, especially our seminarian candidates, so that we shall continue to answer the call of conversion to Jesus, the call of faith and understand the necessity of repentance for the forgiveness of our sins.

"New Courage"
PENTECOST SUNDAY
Acts 2:1-11

All Christians call today Pentecost Sunday, fifty days after Easter, when we celebrate God's presence among us, known as the Holy Spirit. It is a good day for the celebration of the Sacrament of Confirmation, especially for adults.

We know the story of the first coming of the Holy Spirit. After the Ascension the apostles were gathered in the upper room with Mary. We are told that they were frightened and nervous. There was a great miracle – tongues of fire came and descended upon their heads, there was a rushing wind. An equal miracle is that they went out to preach the gospel. They were heard in many tongues but it was one message then and it is the same message now, two thousand years later.

The world was then much more hostile to Christianity than it is now. Roman society was more cruel and oppressive, many were slaves. People were killed in the games fighting one another or fighting animals. Family life was much more chaotic, women had no rights. Sexual oppression was rampant. The simple message of the Church spread steadily and slowly through the example, the love and the preaching of the followers of Christ, despite hardship, hostility and recurrent persecution.

We Christians still start from a few simple beliefs. There is only one triune God, spiritual not material, Creator and Sustainer of the universe. St. Patrick preached about one shamrock with three leaves; or tradition tells us he did! This God is good, interested in us enough to love each one of us, even the most unlovable! So he sent his only Son to live with us, teach us, suffer and die for us. First of all the one true God acts through his Church, the Catholic Church and then the other Christian churches and communities.

The Spirit of God is also active in the world, not usually through prophets and heroes, but through everyday events and persons, which we often take for granted. We depend on the yearly seasons, night and day, good weather and rains, just as the Spirit works whenever men and women freely choose the good, the true and the beautiful. The struggle against evil and selfishness, the struggle for meaning and faith are inspired by the Spirit.

In faith we know God is near, but the Spirit is elusive, sometimes hard to recognise with our minds and feel in our hearts.

All of us should want to understand what is happening around us and, more importantly, to hear and understand as we "listen to what the Spirit is saying to the churches" (Rev. 3:22). This is hard work and public opinion is sometimes quite wrong, often contributing to a culture of death and disarray. As adults we all have to choose; good or evil, faith or fear.

The Spirit must not be reduced to the blind, impersonal forces which guide the universe and occasionally seem to fail, e.g., in earthquakes, volcanoes, droughts, because the Holy Spirit is personal, the Third Person of the Trinity, the Spirit of Jesus Christ, our leader and redeemer. Only a personal God can love us.

Yes, the Holy Spirit is mysterious, invisible and in some ways silent. Scripture speaks of the Spirit as "ruah", breath or wind. Discerning what the Holy Spirit wants us to do requires courage, since it sometimes means going where we do not wish to go.

The Father is the source of all love. The Son is light from light, true God from true God. He came down amongst us to be born of his mother Mary but with no human father. The Spirit of love from the Father and the Son is sometimes referred to as the "go-between God", God amongst us, God in our hearts, the Holy Spirit.

This is not a primitive mythology. It is based in the scriptures. It has been refined by the great Councils of the fourth and the fifth century. The Church in the creeds and in the central teachings of scripture says what She means and means what She says. It is not something to be deconstructed away. It is not one of a long list of puzzles that can be put aside.

Our language is not perfect but it can take us towards God because we see the goodness of God in the creation around us. God is neither male nor female. God is spirit. Often in asking the grade Sixes who are to be confirmed what they mean when they say that God is spirit, we eventually come up with all sorts of analogies: X-rays, TV rays, the force of gravity.

All these are very real, very powerful and quite invisible. What I say to the children is that the best place to start to understand the mystery of God is to think of their parents' love for them. Very real, very powerful, absolutely necessary but quite invisible except in its effects. God is love. The Trinity is a great mystery of love.

This mystery of love, this God, is truly with us today, just as the Holy Spirit was at the Feast of Pentecost, the first Pentecost. He is present in many ways. In all the good things that happen in life but especially through the mystery of the Church and through the Sacraments. That is one reason why we surround the Sacraments with special signs of devotion and respect.

In good times the fruits of the Spirit exist in abundance, but when the spirit of evil strengthens, these fruits are in short supply. St. Paul listed them to the Galatians as love, joy, peace, patience, kindness, goodness, trustfulness gentleness and self-control. However in every circumstance we need to cooperate, because no one has all the gifts and every person is obliged to search for the truth that Jesus is Lord. The same Spirit works in different ways in different persons.

No one has any right to opt out of the search for truth, especially in faith and morals, no matter how limited or deep their level of religious understanding.

Some people are inclined to search only for what is "true for them", leaving others also to make their choices of what is true. They value their right to pick and choose. But there is another important consideration. If personal choice constitutes morality, no one can tell you you're acting wrongly. It is only your critic's point of view! In faith and morals it's up to the individual to decide which claims are true, they claim.

This sounds attractive as long as we acknowledge that we find and recognise truths in faith and morals as well as science; we do not create truths.

The earth does not become flat because I deny that it is spherical. Laws of physics are discovered, often understood imperfectly, but not created by human minds. God does not come into existence because I believe in Him (neither does the man in the moon), nor would He cease to exist if I became an unbeliever.

No adult should ever opt out of the search for truth, especially in faith and morals. It is important to know that God loves us, to know the difference between right and wrong, to know that love is supremely important.

I ask all those who are uncertain about God's existence, or uncertain about claims to truth, to pray each day: *Dear God of Love, if You exist, bring me to the Truth.*

How can we condemn evil if moral truths are simply a matter of opinion? Surely the slaughter of the innocent, rape, drug running and many other crimes cannot be defined out of existence?

Peer pressure can be fierce, whether we are young or old. Alcohol, drugs and pornography can seem attractive escapes for every generation. Money and power still glitter for a good number. Long journeys start with small steps and bad habits capture our wills. Apathy is poisonous, but individual courage and leadership inspire others, like a snowball rolling down a hill.

When the Holy Spirit first came upon the timid disciples at Pentecost, they were transformed, filled with the spirit of courage.

Peter, the up-country Galilean who had denied Christ three times, supported now by the Eleven, went out and preached to the Jewish visitors to Jerusalem from many nations that Jesus the Nazarene whom they had crucified was back from the dead, raised to life and freed from the pangs of Hades. Three thousand were converted and baptised (Acts 2:1-41).

Mindful of this abrupt change, this remarkable conversion, we should acknowledge again that following Christ must make a difference to our lives and therefore to the society in which we live. If there seems to be no difference, if the lives of Christians are completely indistinguishable from the lives of surrounding non-believers, then there is something basically wrong.

Over the years I have sometimes mentioned Evelyn Waugh, a marvellous English writer from the last century and a convert to Catholicism. He was received into the Church by Father

Martin D'Arcy, then a well-known Jesuit at Oxford University. Unfortunately Waugh was sometimes, perhaps even often, cruel and cranky. Someone asked him how he could be a Catholic and behave so badly. He replied by asking the speaker to imagine how much worse he would have been if not a Catholic. It is not a bad reply, but he obviously needed considerably more repair work; repentance, forgiveness, the slow development of good habits.

Just as the original event of Pentecost transformed the apostles from a group in the cenacle that was afraid of the Jewish authorities into a group of brave and enthusiastic preachers, so too we must pray that our lives and our words will also witness to the death and resurrection of the Lord.

God the Holy Spirit is still with us, at work on us and among us. We must believe this.

"The Body and Blood of Christ"
FEAST OF CORPUS CHRISTI
Gen 14:18-20; 1 Cor 11:23-26;
Gospel: Luke 9:11-17.

Corpus Christi is a Latin term for the Body of Christ. This feast celebrates a New Testament truth; that Jesus meant what he said when he prayed over the bread and wine "This is my Body, This is my Blood" at the Last Supper, the first celebration of the Eucharist.

This is the first aspect we must stress on this feast – the miraculous presence of Jesus Christ in the host. "Visus, tactus, gustus fallitur" as St. Thomas wrote. All our senses are deceived, our sight, our touch, our taste. The repetition of the miracle should not blind us to its importance.

But we celebrate this ancient truth in a thoroughly Catholic way through a medieval feast which came into Church life after the urgings of Blessed Juliana of Liege in Belgium about 1230. Later that century Pope Urban IV endorsed the feast and it was made universal in the Church during the fourteenth century. On many occasions it is celebrated with a public procession like today's.

Often when speaking with primary school children from the middle or senior years (years 3 and 4 to year 6) I ask them why the priest does not use coke and a pizza or some Australian equivalent such as lemonade and a piece of cake rather than bread and wine. I explain to the children that the Church is occasionally criticised for being old-fashioned and perhaps in a youth Mass the Church could try to update its image, appear more "with it" by trying some such strategy. To my relief this suggestion is nearly always greeted with laughter, followed by silence as they venture reasons why this change would be unacceptable. They often begin by pointing out that the bread and wine become the Body of Christ and I further explain that the proposal is that some other materials, used as food today, would be substituted as the basic material for the miracle.

On every occasion some child has been able to explain fairly early in the dialogue that Jesus used bread and wine at the Last Supper and because the priest and people are celebrating this same Eucharist, we follow Christ's example. Even in those countries where rice is eaten more frequently than bread, we must follow the example of the Lord. This position is not open to change.

Actually Jesus himself chose an Old Testament practice, which we heard of in the first reading, used by Melchizedek the King of Salem and priest of the Most High God. Abraham is our father in faith, in many ways the founder of the monotheist tradition, and Melchizedek, also a monotheist who acknowledged the God Most High as creator of heaven and earth, used bread and wine when he blessed Abraham. We belong to an ancient tradition, which Our Lord developed and expanded, going back more than 3,700 years.

We need food for our life's journey and activity in order to produce energy, just as the followers of Jesus who followed him into the countryside were hungry. A balanced diet, not too much, not too much of the wrong foods like fat and sugar, keeps us healthy, able to work, enjoy ourselves, and be happy.

So too we need regular prayer and worship if our faith is to be strong and if we want to be able to do the right thing regularly; if we want to be able to acknowledge we are sinners and ask forgiveness of God and if we want our faith to remain strong.

Faith is more like learning to play a musical instrument or learning a foreign language than buying a house or a car. While we have to maintain our houses, they do not disappear if they are neglected, but take a long time to deteriorate. On the other hand if we never use our musical ability or practise a foreign language, we can lose the ability almost completely.

So too in daily life we need to exercise, to work, to spend our energy. If we stupidly did nothing at all in order to conserve our energy, our laziness would ensure we became weaker and weaker. Popular wisdom proclaims "Use it or lose it".

Following Christ is very similar to this. We need to be doing the correct thing regularly in order to remain genuinely Catholic and we need to keep up our energy through prayer.

In many ways Catholics have moved into the mainstream of Australian life and some of us do not want to be thought of as different from majority Australia. So we can become diffident, reluctant to stand-up for our Catholic principles even in everyday conversations. The enemies of Christian influence in public life are working in a similar direction to exclude Christian values from public discussion. We should not be helping them. But courage and knowledge are needed so we can speak up effectively.

For all these reasons a public procession through the streets of Sydney is an important witness to our belief in the real presence of Jesus in the Eucharist, but also an important symbol reminding us of the necessity of defending and charitably explaining Catholic principles in our daily life, in our families, while we are at work and among our friends.

Discipleship always comes at some cost. Following Christ is

never cost free, even when there is no or little official hostility. For some personalities it is easier to rise to defend the Church against hostility, than it is to rebut the charge that we are old fashioned, a bit ridiculous or superstitious. We need new ways to explain all truths, but we still need age-old virtues like courage, prudence and courtesy to explain our basic claims and truths.

We know of beautiful truths. We believe that the eternal Word became man, took flesh of the Virgin Mary and lived among us. Stranger still the main event in his life, which Jesus highlighted for our memorial celebrations, was his death on the cross, when he gave up his life for us. As St. Paul explained to the people of Corinth, on every occasion when we eat this bread and drink this cup we celebrate the death of the Lord, as a slave on the cross, until He comes again.

Neither does the strangeness end here, because the New Testament teaches that Jesus is not among us simply as a fond memory but under the forms of bread and wine, which we eat so that the elements become part of our own body. We worship and adore the Host in the monstrance and in our tabernacles, but the Eucharist was instituted to be eaten, as food for our journey. We stand before a series of great mysteries.

In the words of today's sequence, the *Lauda Sion*:
> *This faith to Christian men is given –*
> *Bread is made flesh by words from heaven:*
> *Into his blood the wine is turned ...*
> *Concealed beneath the two-fold sign,*
> *Meet symbols of the gift divine.*

This is our faith. We thank God for it.

"Unworthy but Faithful"
9TH SUNDAY IN ORDINARY TIME
1 Kings 8:41-3; Gal 1:1-2, 6-10;
Gospel: Luke 7:1-10.

In 2011 the churches in the English-speaking world introduced the long awaited new Mass translation of the third edition of the Roman Missal replacing the version which had been in use for about forty years.

The new translation had been endorsed by each of the national bishops' conferences (a two-thirds majority in a secret ballot was required) as nearly ten years of work came to completion after the Holy See's mandating the project in the 2001 Instruction *Liturgiam Authenticam*. This instruction followed the recognition and decision of Blessed John Paul II in 1997 that the liturgical translations in many languages needed improvement.

In the Mass when the host is held up by the priest for adoration and described as "the Lamb of God who takes away the sins of the world", the congregation now replies with the words, "Lord, I am not worthy that you should enter under my roof, but only say the word and my soul shall be healed."

This is completely faithful to the Latin original and a development on the earlier simplified English version "Lord, I am not worthy to receive you, but only say the word and I shall be healed".

This new translation restates the beautiful sentiments of the centurion in today's gospel passage, who wanted Jesus to heal his servant.

On a number of occasions Luke's accounts are not found in the other gospels. Much of the limited knowledge we have of Jesus' early life comes only from Luke, but this story of the centurion is also told by Matthew and probably by John.

The stories do not accord in significant details, which is usually a good indication that the authors are striving to tell the truth. Neither should we underestimate the difficulties in obtaining the truth in a society where there were no newspapers, no radio and television, no internet. Today we struggle with too much information, some of it designed to deceive. The problems of two thousand years ago were quite different and the evangelists were often not much concerned about historical accuracy in specifics which were tangential to their main theological points.

All three versions agree that the incident occurred in Capernaum, while John has the supplicant as a "royal official" rather than a centurion. John also differs from the others in calling the child "a son" rather than a servant and does not recount the centurion's comments on the exercise of authority, replacing it with a brief discussion on the importance of signs and portents. Some of the commentators believe John's source on this cure was distinct from that used by Luke and this seems likely.

Capernaum was the village we might describe as the base for Jesus' preaching activities. Peter certainly lived there and the present Church has been developed in three stages over the centuries around his house. Some have conjectured that Jesus was welcomed in their synagogue, because Capernaum was on a trade route from the east and the locals were more open to "different" approaches to theology.

Despite this initial welcome, Our Lord finished up condemning the village, as he did with Nazareth, because of their lack of faith.

The remains of the original synagogue, the largest in Galilee, date only from the fourth or fifth century A.D., so we cannot claim that Jesus taught in that building, although it is probably the original site.

Obviously the centurion, a Roman commander in charge of one hundred soldiers, was not Jewish. He was a God-fearing man, a sympathiser with the Jewish religion who had built the synagogue for them. He initially asked the local Jewish elders to approach Jesus on behalf of his servant. He continued to feel himself unworthy of such a miracle, so he then asked some friends to speak to the Lord, but he never wavered in his faith that Jesus was able to help. Jesus had only to give the command and his servant would be healed. It is not surprising that the Lord commended his faith, and remarked that he had found nothing to equal it in the house of Israel.

Luke's gospel was also written for the gentiles, people like ourselves who are not Jewish. We sometimes forget that all the first Christians were Jewish, or at least from the Middle East, until Paul baptised in Philippi Lydia "of the purple dye trade", the first European convert. Luke's Greek-speaking gentile readers would have been consoled and encouraged by the faith of our man, a Roman and a soldier; neither characteristic endeared him to the Jews!

In Luke's gospel particularly, many of those who believed and those who were commended were either disreputable or foreigners. Jesus' apostles were Jewish, but the message was designed for outsiders and increasingly they answered the invitation.

Do we now have in Australia a somewhat parallel situation, where many of the "older" Australians, descended from the Irish or intermarried with the British, seem to be less and less interested in Christ and the Catholic tradition? In many parishes most of our parishioners are recent migrants or the children of migrants.

I regularly explain that the most difficult constituency we have now, especially among the middle aged even more than among the young, are the "blue eyes," often known as the Anglos, less often by the more accurate term Anglo-Celts. In so many cases good parents who provided good education have seen their children drift away, so that some of the grandchildren are not even baptised. Too many of those invited to the feast are too busy with other things to come. We should pray and strive to change this.

Let us pray for our own faith and aim to keep it nourished through prayer and good works. And let us pray that through our efforts at re-evangelisation more and more outsiders, like the Roman centurion, will want to join us and worship Christ, the Son of God.

"Resurrections"
10TH SUNDAY IN ORDINARY TIME B
1 Kings 17:17-24; Gal 1:11-19;
Gospel: Luke 7.11-16.

This morning's reading which tells how Jesus raised the widow of Naim's son from the dead is found only in the Gospel of Luke the physician. Naturally this happening would have been of special interest to him. As in the Gospel story of two weeks ago, when Jesus healed the ten lepers, we see how the Lord was moved by human suffering, and acted to lessen it, just as we too must do so, in different ways today.

But Luke intended the story to have a more profound significance than this. The whole incident has a close similarity with a miracle performed by Elijah, and recounted in the 1st and 2nd Book of Kings. We also find important differences, because Jesus brought the boy back to life without any difficulty. Elijah was forced to try a couple of times, as the first attempt by his disciple Giezi was unsuccessful. Elijah then took personal charge of the situation, and with much difficulty and with the help of practices very similar to mouth-to-mouth resuscitation techniques used today, and similar to the magic practices of his own time, he succeeded in inducing the boy to breathe again.

Luke was the most polished of the New Testament writers and the most conscious stylist, and he certainly intended to emphasise Jesus' unique role. The Jews believed that when the Messianic kingdom was inaugurated, the Spirit of Elijah himself would return.

Luke wanted to show that Christ had this spirit and more, because He was not merely a prophet, but Son of God.

Above and beyond this too, the incident prefigures Christ's resurrection from the dead, and the time when we too shall rise body and soul. In the first centuries, the most emphasised belief of the early Church was the resurrection.

The Acts of the Apostles tell us that the apostles were the "witnesses" of the resurrection – they lived their belief in the Risen Christ, the symbol of their hope, and of the victory over sin. Today, we don't dwell much on the Resurrection – certainly not on our own personal Resurrection. We believe in it, but we don't like to discuss it, because we aren't sure what it means – and anyhow, it can provoke fear and embarrassment. Actually, however, there is no truth which coincides better with all that is good in the modern world, and there is no truth which gives greater consistency to so much of our modern efforts.

We know from Paul's letters to the Ephesians and Colossians, from Peter's second epistle, from the Apocalypse that at the end of time there will be a "new heaven and a new earth", when the whole cosmos will be transfigured and renewed with humanity at its crown. It is comforting to believe that in some mysterious way all genuine human achievement and goodness will be distilled into and preserved in this new supernatural Christocentric universe.

The Son of God took on our human nature. Material creation is good. The ancient Greek philosophy, which emphasised the immortality of the soul and was sometimes tempted to see the body as inferior or even as a prison of the spirit, is in strong contrast with Christian perspectives.

Even today some mistaken people strive to escape the limitations of their bodies, or their difficult personal circumstances by losing themselves in drugs and in alcohol. They find no escape in this direction but only grim prisons of darkness and sometimes despair.

When we rise from the dead in body and soul, through the redemptive power of Christ Our Lord, we shall bring with us the capacities for faith, hope and love we have developed during our lifetimes. But we will rise through the redemptive power of Christ, not like the widow's son to an extended human life, but to the eternal happiness of heaven.

"Forgiveness"

11TH SUNDAY IN ORDINARY TIME
2 Sam 12:7-10. 13; Gal 2:16. 19-21;
Gospel: Luke 7:36-8:3.

All three readings today talk about the great Christian mystery of forgiveness, which we are apt to take for granted until we make a big mistake ourselves and want forgiveness, or are called to forgive others in some serious matter.

Forgiveness was a reality in the Old Testament story of David, but the penance or punishment of continuing strife for David's family and descendants was fierce. In the New Testament Jesus' teaching of forgiveness is more developed and central, linked with the concepts of love (obviously) and perhaps less obviously with faith. But we need faith to believe God can and will forgive us.

The Gospel story of the prostitute greeting Jesus is prefaced by Jesus' teaching on love and forgiveness and by the beatitudes. Then follow four examples of love in action: a) the cure of the centurion's son; b) the resurrection of the son of the widow of Nain; c) the preaching of John the Baptist; and d) Jesus with the prostitute.

Simon the Pharisee was a serious man, who probably took himself even more seriously. Not a mocker or trickster, he invited Jesus to a meal, not to set Jesus up and demolish him, but because he was interested, perhaps half believing. He respected Jesus sufficiently to call him "rabbi" or teacher.

At oriental banquets, guests left their sandals at the door and reclined on couches with their feet behind them. It sounds most uncomfortable, especially if you had a bad back! Normally doors were left open for visitors to wander in, beggars for food, the inquisitive, perhaps students to listen.

Although Mary Magdalene is mentioned almost immediately after this excerpt, this is not sufficient to identify her with the prostitute, the public sinner. We have no evidence that Jesus knew the visitor. She was simply someone who had heard him, or at least heard his message, and changed her ways. She decided to thank him with this magnificent public gesture by washing his feet with expensive ointment. We should contrast this with the aloof and formal welcome Jesus had received earlier from Simon, no foot bath, no kiss, no perfume, the polite "don't call me, I'll call you approach"; and the public scandal only deepened when the woman dried Our Lord's feet with her hair, apparently something no decent woman would then do in public.

Simon knew the woman's reputation and was scandalised by Jesus' reaction. Surely Jesus must have recognised this woman for what she was; why didn't he fob her off?

But Our Lord moved in a direction Simon never expected with the story of the two debtors and the comparison between the two welcomes. He concluded by telling this woman her sins were forgiven because of her faith and her love.

This is a beautiful incident, like some of Our Lord's parables, which tells us a thousand times more than a hundred pages of dry talk about forgiveness.

Many persons can forgive easily but most of us find it hard in extreme situations. Nature is much less forgiving. We remember the old saying: "God always forgives; men and women sometimes forgive, but nature never forgives". In 2010 I spoke to some hundreds of young adults at Theology on Tap on "The Costs of Discipleship". Conscientious young Christians today know how they have to resist the neo-pagan influences that surround them. It is not easy and they often feel isolated. Cut-price Christianity is hazardous and if we are regularly slow to pay the costs of discipleship, we are more likely to need God's forgiveness in some big way. King David is an example of this. Despite his achievements and the many blessings given to him, he had become vain and arrogant, a victim to his passions. At the other extreme the woman who anointed Jesus' feet was only at the beginning of her conversion story.

The need to repent, the call to conversion, are constants as we go through life, not just at the beginning of the story. We need humility as well as perseverance, even if we are closer to the end than the beginning. Everyone who stands should beware lest he fall!

God's grace and love are all different from the wages of sin; different even from the forgiveness Mahatma Gandhi required, as depicted in a film from many years ago. After the post-Independence riots in India between Hindus and Muslims, a Hindu, who had laid aside his chopper, told Gandhi "I am damned to Hell because I killed a young child, crushed his skull on the pavement". "There is a way out", Gandhi replied. "Take a young orphan and bring him up as your own. But make sure he is a Muslim and bring him up as a Muslim!"

This is a beautiful story, but the penance is terribly stiff. Would the killer's Hindu neighbours allow him to bring up a Muslim? Would the child be accepted into a Muslim congregation?

Christ, as Son of God, offers us another way out of hell. The Sacrament of reconciliation, or confession through the priest, is the usual way for us today. For many acts, a murder for example, only God can forgive because the victim is gone.

Forgiveness is one of the most beautiful gifts given to us by Christ and the Church. We should never take it for granted, as those brought up as Christians are tempted to do. As I tell the youngsters, even Hitler or Stalin could be forgiven if they repented. God will forgive us, even when we cannot forgive ourselves! We should thank God for this.

"The Divine Redeemer"

12TH SUNDAY IN ORDINARY TIME
Zech. 12:10-11; 13:1; Gal. 3:26-29;
Gospel: Luke 9:18-24.

Some years ago a leading left-of-centre metropolitan newspaper had an article where the author wondered whether the idea of God has been wired into us by evolution and was transmitted through our genes. This was not a new claim.

The minority of people who deny the reality of the spiritual and are materialists have a problem in the fact that religious belief has been almost universal in all cultures and throughout history. Western Europe today is unique in history for the high percentage, still a minority in most countries, who do not believe in God.

If we are able to pray the psalm refrain honestly "my soul is thirsting for you, O Lord my God", then we are in good company with the overwhelming majority of believers throughout history, although many originally were not monotheists, not believers in one God.

While I believe in personal freedom, I would not be surprised if human nature did possess a predisposition, which encouraged us not only to search for meaning, but to search for God.

Some of our contemporaries are like the author of the article cited; they do not feel obliged to worship God, or subscribe to any set of beliefs about a supreme Being, but cannot let go of the idea of God completely.

As Catholics we need more than sincerity, more than a vague interest in religion, more than a set of questions. We follow the God of Abraham, Isaac and Jacob, who is the father of Our Lord Jesus Christ.

As Catholic Christians, we follow Christ because we believe He provided the answers to the central problems and questions of life. Moreover He came among us, lived with us, taught us and suffered and died to redeem us.

After nearly 300 years of intermittent persecution, in 313 A.D. Christians in the Roman Empire obtained religious freedom. The emperor Constantine the Great hoped Christians would bring unity, but in the early years of freedom for the Catholic church in the fourth and fifth centuries there were terrible doctrinal and political conflicts, complete sometimes with riots and strife and ongoing divisions, as the Church clarified the doctrine of the Trinity and especially as the full divinity of Christ was defended against those who denied He was divine or claimed He was only semi-divine. Arius, an influential priest from Alexandria in Egypt, then the leading theological centre, publicly denied Jesus' divinity.

The answers to Jesus' question in today's Gospel "who do the crowds say I am" have been many and various over the years and remain various today also, where a goodly number of Christians do not accept Christ's divinity. So too opinion was divided in those first days in the general discussion provoked by his teaching and miracles. As I have explained many times enormous consequences follow when we accept that Christ is truly divine. Above all Christ's divinity affects the status of His teachings and the reality of redemption.

Just recently after I had preached in a parish, a catechist wrote to me explaining that her pupils understood that Christ was very special, a wonderful son of God, but did not realise He was fully divine as well as human, the Eternal Word, the equal of the Father and the Spirit in the Trinity. She wanted me to make this point more explicitly and regularly.

It is interesting that Peter's confession that Jesus is the Christ of God, i.e., the one anointed with the oil of chrism (Christ is not a family name like Jones or O'Brien or Alfredo or Nguyen) and therefore the Messiah, is immediately followed by Christ's first prophecy that he was destined to suffer grievously be rejected and put to death.

Luke does not mention, as Matthew and Mark do, that Peter objected to Christ's prediction of his own suffering and was rebuked for his misdirected concern!

We are used to the crucifixion story, but that conjunction of messianic vocation, of divine dignity and ignominious suffering was upsetting and baffling to the disciples. I often quote the Muslim taxi driver who said he could not believe in a God who was so weak. To make matters worse Jesus continued on immediately and said that his followers will also have to suffer.

What does it mean to say that we must renounce ourselves, take up our cross every day; that if we want to save our life we must lose it?

These are provocative and profound teachings, worth prayer and puzzling.

Perhaps the first part of the answer is that if we put ourselves first at the expense of those around us we are not following the commandment to love others. This cannot bring us to heaven and it cannot bring us to peace and contentment in daily living either.

To follow the commandments, to respect and help others regularly, to pray daily and go to weekly Mass, all cost us something. They do not represent the easy way out.

Sometimes in our daily life, at work or with our social acquaintances, we shall be disadvantaged because of our Christian principles. Sometimes it is unpopular to tell the truth or to call a spade a spade, however politely, when we insist some activities are wrong. Sometimes it needs courage to resist abortion, to maintain Christian standards of sexual morality before marriage. All this and more constitutes taking up our cross to follow Christ.

Jesus is not John the Baptist, nor Elijah, nor one of the prophets. He is not another great philosopher, not a poet or scholar, not a priest or bishop or pope. Jesus is God's only Son, fully divine as well as fully human. Because of this He brings us the Maker's instructions. We can trust Him as our Saviour and Teacher.

He is worth following as he calls us to take up our cross, but he has promised us one hundred fold rewards and eternal life for the sacrifices we make.

"No Fire and Brimstones"
13TH SUNDAY IN ORDINARY TIME
1 Kg 19:16, 19-21; Gal 5:1,13-18;
Gospel: Luke 9:51-62.

We all belong in different ways to the story of successive generations as we are part of the history or tradition of our family, perhaps our Church and different local, national, even international communities.

Our awareness of this varies from individual to individual and is also different at different stages of our lives. When we are young we usually do not worry much about these issues and cannot wait to grow up. Often when I ask young primary school children their age, they reply, "I will be nine next birthday". "Oh", I say, "that means you are now eight years old." Sometimes they are running this line six or even nine months before their next birthday!

One of the blessings of a reasonably happy childhood is that children are focused on the future, persons of hope and optimism, and our task as adults is to support them in this optimism.

Many individuals become more aware of their part in the human chain at the birth of their children. What values or truths will they pass on, what virtues will they teach to their children? Often they identify gaps in their own childhood and want to remedy them for their children. In other areas they will strive to do exactly as their parents did; in some cases they will make explicit changes. A cousin from interstate once called to see me with his wife and children. They like camping holidays but in our brief conversation their teenage son explained to me that he liked travelling, but not the sort of holidays favoured by his parents.

When, like myself, you have completed many decades, when some of your contemporaries have retired and most are grandparents, your perspective changes and you consider the future life after your contribution has finished. What will follow? What might I still be able to do to help the situation in the future, given that the past is already written in stone?

What do we envisage for the Catholic Church in the coming generations? Will we be able to continue to produce and maintain lively communities of faith, love and service? Is the Lord regarded as a valuable part of our inheritance?

I hope we are coming out of a period when not just old people, who are always tempted to think many things were better in their childhood, but also young people were resigned to the conclusion that Christianity would be radically weaker in the future. No such decline is inevitable. Certainly it is not what we want. In fact it is a situation we are determined to avoid through faith, prayer, hard work and a commitment to be open to God's grace. But the future will only develop in this way if sufficient numbers of young people are like Elisha, from the first Book of Kings, who rose and followed Elijah and became his servant after Elijah was told by the Lord to anoint Elisha as his successor and throw his cloak over him.

Elijah from the ninth century B.C. is an important figure. A few of you might even remember me saying he is of particular importance because belief in the one true God was nearly obliterated in his time among the Jewish people. A primary struggle with young people today is to show them through our lives and convince them from our teaching that the one true God exists and loves them, and then to explain that the answer they give to the call of the one true God expressed through Christ his Son has immense consequences for them in this life and the life to come. God is not an optional extra to a good moral life and community standards. Concern for the poor and disadvantaged, for the family, for the unborn and unemployed would be very different without belief in God, in the ten commandments and in a final universal judgement. It was those who loved God, believed in the first great commandment to love God, whose lives convinced public opinion that the second great commandment to love one another was correct.

In today's gospel passage from St. Luke, which seems to be a collection of various bits and pieces of Jesus' story, we hear of Jesus calling some to follow him and warning a volunteer that the Christian path is not a bed of roses. "Foxes have holes and the birds of the air have nests, but the Son of Man has nowhere to lay his head."

All individuals who have some influence in making appointments, in choosing some rather than others to particular offices or roles in any work in progress, might take consolation from Our Lord's record in appointing the twelve apostles. One out of the twelve, went wrong, Judas Iscariot, who betrayed him.

In two of the small incidents recounted here we cannot be sure how the story turned out, but both started badly and might have ended there. The seed seems to have fallen on rocky ground and not caught at all.

The first gentleman invited to follow Jesus replied, not unreasonably, that he had to bury his father before he joined up. "Leave the dead to bury their dead" was the abrupt reply he received. I suspect the reason he gave as an excuse was not entirely true, while the man who wanted to say goodbye to his family was told that he should not be looking back, but concentrating on his work for the Kingdom. Like so many today they might have wanted to keep their options open. But one act of commitment is worth one hundred options.

Jesus knew that many are reluctant to give a direct "no", but seek excuses for delay, for slipping away quietly and less obviously.

James and John were known as the "sons of thunder"; obviously they were hot-headed. But their response was wrong to call down fire from heaven to consume the Samaritan town which did not welcome Jesus. The Samaritans were Jews, but deep hostility existed between the two groups, because the Samaritans had fought with Jewish enemies and did not believe in worshipping at the Temple in Jerusalem. For most of us the first reason would have been paramount, but for the Jews worshipping in the Temple was enormously important.

God has a plan for each of us, which respects our free will and which is sometimes difficult to discover. However this plan is usually recognised when we feel we are contributing, reasonably happy and acting appropriately in the succession of the generations. That is why we believe in God's providence, not simply coincidence. May we all have the wisdom to recognise and the courage to answer God's call in the unfolding story of our family, our Church and the different local communities to which we belong.

"Written in the Book of Life"
14TH SUNDAY IN ORDINARY TIME
Isaiah 66:10-14; Gal 6:14-18;
Gospel: Luke 10:1-12.17-20.

Luke was probably not one of the seventy two disciples sent out on mission by Our Lord although he is the only evangelist to recount the incident. All the evangelists tell of the sending out of the Twelve on mission.

Luke certainly intended to compare this with Moses, the lawgiver, appointing seventy elders to help him govern and share his prophetic gifts. As the Twelve represent the twelve tribes of Israel the seventy-two probably represent all the nations. The gospel texts are divided on whether the number was 70 or 72, whether Moses' number was followed exactly or a multiple of 12.

This is not a twenty-first century text and we should take some consolation from it. Even in Our Lord's time, nearly 2000 years ago, the labourers were few although the harvest was rich. By any standards Christ and his followers had small beginnings. We need a special effort of imagination to picture this tiny group of disciples in a violently hostile environment with no network of parishes, schools or hospitals, no government support. They only had faith, hope and love, but it was more than enough. Jesus asks his followers to pray for labourers, to gather the harvest.

Our Lord's instructions to his disciples are provocative, interesting and unusual because they are to go as lambs among wolves. This is certainly not a military metaphor although the prophecy about the wolves was justified by nearly 300 years of persecution in the Roman Empire. Nor are persecutions simply a distant memory for us because there were more Christian martyrs in the twentieth century than in any other. Most people today are not aware of this.

Jesus' practice of sending two together for mission work was followed in the Early Church as we see in Paul and Barnabas and then Paul and Silas (after the difficulties with Barnabas) and Peter and John. Members of the Neo-Catechumenal Way still go out preaching and witnessing in pairs.

Jesus' requirements are fierce and uncomfortable because the disciples are to wear no sandals and carry no haversack or purse. Since they were going into Samaria, which was religiously hostile, the injunction against greeting or saluting any one was probably a prudential recommendation. When they are welcomed they are to take the hospitality offered and not search for better accommodation.

The temptation for every age is to reshape Jesus into its own image and today many Christian fellow-travellers and a considerable number of Christians would not have an image of a Christ, who threatened evil consequences for those who rejected his message. Not only are the disciples to display publicly their displeasure when they are rejected, but when the Kingdom arrives the unbelievers' punishment will be worse than Sodom's.

The curses of Jesus on the unrepentant and unbelieving villages of Chorazim, Bethsaida and Capernaum are omitted from today's reading, but these towns are derelict ruins even now.

Eternal consequences follow from accepting or knowingly rejecting Jesus as I explained to a couple of groups of young adults travelling through the Holy Land, when we visited these dismal sites. I told them that it doesn't pay to mess with God!

The disciples returned rejoicing at the good reception they had received and at their power over the Evil One. "I have seen Satan fall like lightning from heaven", Jesus explained. But He said they should not rejoice in these spectacular victories, natural and supernatural, but be glad that their names are written in heaven, in the Book of Life (mentioned in Exodus 32:32-3) which records the names and good deeds of the righteous. We still use this model for our books in the Rite of Christian Initiation for Adults (RCIA).

Today as the number of unbelievers slowly increases in Australia we need Catholic leaders in every profession and community, teachers and labourers for an eschatological harvest, for the final Judgement and Victory. Without these volunteers, without those who answer the call, the Church will collapse here.

This is not going to happen as the worst has passed. Religious life vocations are still a challenge, although the New Movements are slowly filling the void and a good number of Australian dioceses have seminarians.

In a religious sense Australia and much of the Western world are running contrary to the patterns in the other continents where the number of Christians is increasing solidly. Most Westerners today do not realise that the percentage of the world's population following one of the great religions is increasing. The world is become more religious! Christ's teaching, when it is lived and taught, is as powerful as it was for the first disciple missionaries. Let us follow Our Lord's advice and "ask the Lord of the harvest to send labourers to his harvest".

"Jesus and the Good Samaritan (i)"
15TH SUNDAY IN ORDINARY TIME
Deut 30:10-14; Col 1:15-20;
Gospel: Luke 10:25-37.

Over the years I have sometimes mentioned an old priest friend of mine, working many years ago in the Mallee in North West Victoria. He rarely prepared his sermons, unfortunately, and he often began by telling the people, "There's not much in these readings."

However, today such a claim would be completely wrong, because we have three beautiful readings, each capable of inspiring a competent sermon.

I would like to begin with the second reading, which is from Paul writing to the Colossians, writing about Christ Jesus, the image of the unseen God and the first born of creation.

Recently I was talking with a few bishops about Church life in Australia and the theological scene in particular, and we agreed that one central point, one pivotal point – a foundational point for Christian life and discussion – is our verdict on who Christ is. Today as in Our Lord's time, enormous consequences follow from the answer that we give to Christ's question, "who do people say that I am?"

If Christ is only another wonderful man, then his teachings are limited by his education and understanding and by the limitations of his culture. And his life and his sufferings are simply another good example of virtue and heroism.

However, if Jesus is divine as well as human, if he has brought us the Maker's instructions because he is the Maker's Son, then he has a unique authority not shared by any human. And I, at least, would not be prepared to claim that I could improve on his teachings, even those ones that are hard and difficult to follow or understand.

Also as the Son of God, his living and especially his suffering and death have special meaning. If we just step outside the Christian framework for a minute, we can understand how devastatingly new and different the idea of a suffering God was to people before Christ. If the Son of God suffered then it is possible of course that he was achieving something infinitely beyond just giving us a good example.

Paul too was concerned with all these issues about who Christ is. For Jesus' contemporaries he was all too human. He was poor, he was uneducated; during his life he was often attacked verbally and ultimately was attacked physically. And another little question for them was how he ranked in comparison with all the angels; what Paul in today's reading called the "thrones and dominations, the sovereignties and powers". This might be less of a concern for us, but Paul responded that all created things, including the angels, were created through Christ.

So Paul was vigorously defending the divinity of Jesus the Son of Mary. This Jesus the Son of Mary existed before all creation, Paul tells us, He holds creation together, He is the head of the Church. Through His Resurrection He is the first born of the Dead and through His death on the Cross he not only gave us an example of courage, of grace under pressure, but reconciled all Creation to God and brought about peace and right order.

We say that Christ redeemed us. Christ couldn't have redeemed us if he was only human. We have many young people here today, and I would like to repeat three points which some of you might have heard me say before. I often explain that all Christians and especially young Christians and Catholics who want to consolidate their faith need to do three things and one of those is to pray regularly outside Sunday Mass. And I suggest that this small passage, the second reading tonight, is a beautiful passage for meditation. Just sitting, having a look at it, reading, thinking about it, praying about it, pondering over it and praying about its claims.

A second necessity for all of us, and, especially young Catholics, is that we have at least some friends who share our views and whom we see regularly. Most of us – especially when we were younger, and I suppose almost as much when we are older – are unable to stand alone forever.

And the third necessity which I want to touch on briefly, and which I mentioned in the introduction, the examination of conscience, is because we need to be doing something, not just talking. I am not criticising anybody here tonight because you are all at Mass and that certainly is doing something and doing something important.

But you might be a little like me and intend to do this and to do that; but also like to talk and like to theorise and sometimes do not get around to doing what we should, perhaps as often and as quickly as we should. And so this is one of the points I believe that our Lord was making when he told the parable of the Good Samaritan to the lawyer.

Now we are told that the lawyer set out to disconcert Jesus, to stir him up. I am tempted to be wicked and say that the lawyer was probably a graduate of Sydney University Law School, well aware of his intelligence and his superior education. Interrogating this religious teacher from the bush, who had no particular educational attainment and might not have been able to write, although we know that Our Lord could read.

It is an interesting question for another time about why Our Lord left us no writings and what consequences follow from this. Probably the lawyer wanted to put Our Lord in his place or as we say he wanted to knock him down a peg or two.

Jesus was up to the challenge and replied with a question, "what does the Law tell you to do?" "Love God, love one another" the lawyer answered and he answered well, but that provoked him into asking a further question, "Who is my neighbour?" And that is often a bad mistake for a lawyer. It was one question too many.

And then we had this marvellous story of the Good Samaritan. Even the question was something of a trap for Jesus, because there were limits on the type of person you were obliged to respect and care for according to Jewish law. Some categories of persons had to be excluded; I think there were certain types of heretics whom you were urged to push into a ditch and then jump on. And the Samaritans in many ways were beyond the pale, too. A person who was sick and who accepted help from a Samaritan could be sent into exile.

The Samaritans were also Jewish. They were monotheists, worshippers of the one true God, who accepted most of the Old Testament writings, but they did not worship at the temple in Jerusalem, and they fought in the past against the Jews and with the Jews' enemies. So there was a long-standing bitterness between the Samaritans and the Jews, that particular type of bitterness which sometimes wells up amongst family members.

In this provocative example of the stranger, the outsider, and despised outsider at that, the Samaritan who helped, Jesus was laying the foundations for the Christian teaching of universal love. However, the point I wish to underline today for present purposes is Our Lord's final words to the lawyer. He said, "Go and do likewise".

Our Lord was saying that good living is not just a matter for endless discussion – much less for point scoring in debate. Good living means that we regularly try to practise what we preach. "Go and do likewise just as the Good Samaritan did".

A little while ago a good friend of mine from interstate who is thinking about becoming a priest said to me that his situation was very complicated. And I said to him, "No, no, in fact that's not true. Your situation is quite simple. The fact is though that the choices that lie before you are hard, difficult choices."

I think many things in life are a little like losing weight; something I have tried to do at some stages more or often less successfully. The solution to losing weight is very, very simple. You eat less and you exercise more. The problem is not finding out what you should do; the problem is that doing it is difficult. At least for some of us it is difficult to do so regularly. I suspect that a deal of Christian living is like that also.

So let us be inspired by Jesus' teaching, let us be inspired by the parable of the Good Samaritan, let us go and do the same ourselves.

"A Second approach to the Good Samaritan (ii)"
15TH SUNDAY IN ORDINARY TIME
Deut 30:10-14; Col 1:15-20;
Gospel: Luke 10:25-37.

We have today the intriguing gospel story of the Good Samaritan, two words we run together automatically because we have heard the gospel many times and the title has entered our Catholic memory and culture. In Melbourne, Australia, we have Good Samaritan College, a high school for boys, and in Sydney we have the Good Samaritan Sisters, founded by Archbishop Polding, our first bishop. Probably there are other institutions so named.

We also know that the Samaritans and Jews were hostile to one another, so that Our Lord telling his Jewish brothers and sisters of a Good Samaritan would be something like him today speaking of a good Palestinian after pointing out that their own Jewish religious leaders had let the side down and done the wrong thing in passing by.

There are many different theories about why the priest and the Levite did travel by without helping. I have read that the priest was preoccupied, either preparing his sermon or distractedly worrying about global warming. More plausibly if the person was dead, contact would have prevented the priest from participating in the ceremonies at the Temple in Jerusalem.

Recently I heard another theory for the first time as one rather acid tongued parishioner told her parish priest that the priest in the parable passed by because he realised that the poor man had been robbed of everything already! I suppose the fact that she was prepared to make the crack in good humour is evidence that all of us as priests could plead not guilty on at least that score.

Recently too I heard of an outspoken Sydney priest from many years ago, who used to explain to his parishioners that it was the bishop who passed by the sufferer without helping and a neighbouring parish priest, whom he disliked, was the Levite! Rumour also has it that the bishop called him in to reprimand him for this creative exegesis, but that did not prevent the parish priest from repeating his theory the next time the text appeared in the cycle of readings.

This story of Our Lord teaches an indelible lesson that boundaries for our Christian love should reach out to everyone we know. It is sometimes easier to like people we do not know, like the humanitarian who loved everyone except most of those he had to live with. Love means an underlying presence of active sympathy, which is expressed in action when there is a need. Just as Christian hope is a virtue sometimes very different from everyday human optimism, so Christian love is different from being naturally friendly and outgoing. People who are naturally a bit unsociable, perhaps they are shy and reserved, can practise Christian love as well as the innately gregarious.

So too this parable reminds us that Christian love can be expressed by people when we do not expect it. This is one important purpose, to force us to broaden our categories, not to write off whole categories of people, not to think badly of individuals, unless the evidence compels us to do so. The kindly Samaritan was a surprise and no doubt every adult here this morning has been surprised and grateful at one time or another by unexpected kindness.

Neither can I resist reminding you of Margaret Thatcher's take on this parable. As politician and Prime Minister of Great Britain she was committed to private initiative and to wealth creation. She pointed out quite correctly that if the Good Samaritan had not been prosperous, with considerable money to spare, he would never have been able to afford to pay for putting the man up in the inn until he was healed. He would not even have been able to afford the wine which he poured into his wounds to cleanse them and the oil he used to hasten the healing process.

Wealth is not an advantage in the Christian scheme of things, because it is the poor or poor in spirit who are blessed according to Jesus, while the rich, however Jesus defined them, have difficulty entering the Kingdom.

It is a good thing for the economy that few of us are either called or strong enough to be perfect by giving away all our possessions. If too many were like Francis of Assisi and gave away everything to live simply the economy would collapse.

But everyone is obliged to earn his money justly and those with wealth in any degree are supposed to use some of it for the poor and disadvantaged. We should pray that the Good Samaritan will inspire many good Catholics throughout the world, and particularly where we have a high standard of living, to follow his example of courage, concern and generosity towards the disadvantaged.

"Mary and Martha"
16TH SUNDAY IN ORDINARY TIME
Genesis 18:1-10; Col 1:24-28;
Gospel: Luke 10:38-42.

Today we have the story of the encounter of Jesus with Martha and Mary. It is a short gospel passage and certainly one that is very well-known. In a homily I preached more than 25 years ago, I claimed that Our Lord's words to Martha were one of his most discussed and difficult sayings. That was probably the reaction of a young busybody. Today as a much older priest and bishop who is regularly looked after with much kindness, it is not surprising that I am much more sympathetic to Mary.

Some would probably still say that Mary is a bit un-Australian; that she should have helped Martha prepare the afternoon tea and then, when everything was ready, the three of them could have sat down for a chat together.

It is interesting that Luke places this incident in the life of Our Lord immediately after the story of the Good Samaritan, where he commends practical help and service; and the story of Martha and Mary is followed by the account of Our Lord giving us the words of the "Our Father" to teach us how to pray.

Jesus told Mary that she had chosen the better part. He did not suggest that what Martha was doing was somehow bad, and I am sure that he enjoyed the meal which she prepared. But what exactly was our Lord commending when he praised Mary's activity?

Whatever the merits of her enterprise, Martha remains an important exemplar of the Christian tradition of hospitality; of offering food and friendship and conversation to friends and strangers, people outside our immediate family situation.

It is a pity that so many meals today are eaten in front of the television, with the family losing an important moment for talk, news and laughter. The mother of one good family I heard of recently, a family with a few children, insisted that the television was turned off during meal time, although the children often objected. As a birthday treat one of the children asked his mother if they could eat their meal in front of the television, like so many other children did!

Obviously hospitality is very stunted and second rate if only food is offered without friendship and conversation. And of course it would be even worse if the guests too were plonked down in front of the television. I supposed we can be grateful that our Lord was not exposed to that particular peril.

Unexpected blessings often follow from acts of kindness, as we saw in the first reading about Abraham, our father in faith. Nearly four thousand years ago, in the hottest part of the day, he offered hospitality to three men who arrived in his tent. I think Marc Chagall, a famous French painter from the last century, has a painting of Abraham extending hospitality to these three heavenly messengers. Perhaps in fact they were angels, a trio who some writers see even as an intimation of the Trinity itself. And when one of the guests was leaving after the hospitality, he promised that Sarah, who had been unable to conceive, would have a son in twelve months time.

It is a little bit of a cliché now but a lovely saying of St. Paul that God rewards the cheerful giver. We might recall in this context that when the disciples were walking to Emmaus with Our Lord after the resurrection, they only recognised who he was after they had invited him in for a meal. At a supernatural level, as well as a human level, hospitality brings its rewards.

To come back to where we were, what was our Lord commending in Mary's role? We should remember that he only praised her after she had been criticised by her sister and had been urged to encourage her to get up and help.

At a human level Our Lord was probably saying that he was enjoying the chat. He might even have felt the need to talk about some of the pressures on him; about some recent encounter with his enemies, or about some equally recent expression of support from his friends and admirers. He was saying that Mary's listening ear, her responses to his conversation, were even more important than preparing the food.

Martha might also have been one of those people who loves to do everything by herself, who likes to go the extra yard, and then complains that everything is left to them. She certainly was a worrier; we have Jesus' words for that. And his response encouraged her to remember once again what was more important.

I am sure that the evangelist Luke saw this encounter as a lesson to us about the importance of prayer. Prayer is not just a formal sequence of words. For the words to have meaning they must come from the heart, and they must be meant. In prayer we have to remember that we are in God's presence; that we are communicating with our brother, who is the Son of God. And we must never forget that this dimension of prayer is vitally important for us personally, for our families and for the Church.

Often those of us who are a bit older worry about our young people, especially if they drift from the regular worship of Sunday Mass. But do we really teach them to pray, encourage them, give them our own personal example, certainly pray with them at Mass, but outside Mass too? Teaching people to pray is not just teaching them the words of prayers. All of us, each one of us, can only learn to pray by praying. We learn on the job, just by doing it. There is no alternative.

Every good community needs plenty of Marthas and plenty of Marys. And perhaps one weakness in the Catholic Church in Australia is that historically we have had plenty of Marthas and not enough Marys. We need prayer, worship, meditation and devotions. We will not retain or develop our strengths unless we realise this.

"Jesus' Prayer"

17TH SUNDAY IN ORDINARY TIME
Gen 18:20-32; Col 2:12-14;
Gospel: Luke 11:1-13.

One of the most important reasons for the existence of the Catholic Church is to teach people to pray; to encourage them to come together each week in Eucharistic communities for the celebration of Sunday Mass and remind them of the obligation to pray personally and regularly.

Prayer is an obligation because God is important. He is our Father who loves us and we should acknowledge this and communicate with him in prayer. Therefore prayer is not just day dreaming, not just an exploration of our psyche, not just an interior journey into an abyss. In fact if we do try to pray regularly, especially with quiet prayer or meditation, we are likely to see our heart of hearts, our soul more accurately, but this is a by-product of opening ourselves to God.

The gospel passage begins with Jesus' followers asking him to teach them to pray, as John the Baptist had taught his disciples. Our Lord responded with most of what we now call the "Our Father," although this Lucan version does not include the prayer that God's will be done on earth as it is in heaven.

Like the Ten Commandments the first two sections are God-centred, as we pray that God's name will be held holy, reverenced and not blasphemed, while the second invocation is that God's Kingdom might come, that goodness and faithfulness might prosper against the world of evil, lies and violence; what Pope John Paul II has called so accurately the culture of death.

Then we are told to pray for ourselves, for our daily needs, for forgiveness of our sins, that we will be able to forgive others and finally we pray that we will not be tested too severely; or as in the words of the Our Father we pray that we may not be led into temptation.

Some superior people over the centuries have told us that we should not ask God for things; that this is immature and perhaps God is too busy with too many people to be listening. It is also true that if God granted some of our prayers it would be to the detriment of others.

I have always replied to that charge by explaining that we are simply following Jesus' instructions to pray for our daily bread, for what we need.

We all know how irritating it is to have a child who is always asking for things. In the old unreconstructed world where I grew up, he was often told that if he kept that up he would receive a present he was not expecting!

There are two extremes to be avoided. If our only prayers to God are prayers of petition, then our faith is shallow and immature. Adults are able to say thanks as well as being grateful and we should thank God for his many blessings. We also need to pray for forgiveness and we should regularly praise God, rejoicing in his goodness and mercy.

There is also an opposite extreme. I regularly explain to secondary students that if they never pray when they are in trouble, it probably means that their faith is non-existent for practical purposes. No one has ever come up later to contradict me on this point.

Today there are two interesting examples of believers making requests of God. In fact in the first reading we have Abraham bargaining with God not to destroy the cities of Sodom and Gomorrah. God originally wanted fifty just men, but settled for ten. If there were ten just men the city would not be destroyed. Ten such men could not be found and the city was destroyed.

It is difficult, indeed impossible, for us now nearly four thousand years later, to identify the core historical truths in this narrative, but it is clear evidence of the continuing Judaeo-Christian moral opposition to homosexual activity. Christians are called to respect everyone and homosexual inclinations are not sinful. But sexual activity, in Christian teaching, is reserved for the marriage of a man and woman.

The second example follows on the Lord's teaching of the Our Father, when he gives an irreverent, almost scandalous example to demonstrate that we should keep on praying even when our prayers are not answered. God, Jesus explained, is a bit like the head of a household in bed with his wife and children, the door barred and bolted, who will eventually answer his friend's request for food, not out of good will, but simply to get rid of him, so that they will be left in peace!

Quite remarkably Jesus urges us to persist in our prayers, because "the one who asks always receives; the one who searches always finds"; the door will be opened to those knocking.

This contradicts much of our experience. Often our prayers do not seem to be answered, at least in our terms.

Many years ago I used to do quite a bit of sports coaching and I was helping to prepare a Year 12 crew for a big race. I had celebrated Mass for the crew, when one of them, an Irish-Australian from a non-practising family, said to us that we should say a decade of the rosary together that we might win. (I have long felt that this was the religious peak or highlight of my coaching career). The inevitable happened and the crew did not win. He came to me in some perplexity afterwards pointing out that we had prayed but still lost!

I said that life was like that, that prayer is never wasted. God certainly hears our prayers; He answers them in some way, sometimes giving what we asked, but not always. In fact he is more likely to reward those with a strong faith and particularly listens to significant prayers e.g. we should always pray for our loved ones.

Jesus explained that God is like a good father who will not give us a snake instead of a fish, nor a scorpion instead of an egg. But he did not claim that God would give us what we seek, only that he would give us the Holy Spirit.

For most of the time, this is more than enough! As St. Augustine said, "Too greedy indeed is he for whom God does not suffice".

"Poverty or Possessions?"
18TH SUNDAY IN ORDINARY TIME
Eccl 1:2, 2:21-23; Col 3:1-5, 9-11;
Gospel: Luke 12:13-21.

Recently I was dipping into St. Ignatius of Loyola's famous Spiritual Exercises, which form the basis of many spiritual retreats today.

I was partially surprised to read again in those pages that St. Ignatius warned especially against pride, possessions and power. He was a master of the spiritual life and the work is a classic; clear headed, tough, demanding and based four-square on the teaching of Christ Our Lord.

I wonder today whether he would add other qualities to the list, like dishonesty, lack of personal discipline. Do the dangers he mentioned cover the problem of sexual weakness, especially in an age of contraception and pornography like today? We can only surmise about this.

But Ignatius' warning against greed follows on directly from today's gospel of Luke, where Jesus refuses to follow the useful practice of many rabbis, who were called on to arbitrate in family disputes on money. He is not going to judge on these matters, but points to the underlying problem. At least one of those in the dispute is likely to have been greedy, rather than motivated by a sense of justice and it is possible that both parties were avaricious.

The passage is found only in Luke's gospel, although we find some parallel in the apocryphal gospel of Thomas, which the Church did not accept as genuinely inspired.

Jesus' message is basic and simple. Possessions are not life. Jesus refused to identify the worth and dignity of human life with possessions. It is much more important to be a person of faith, hope and love, than to be rich and powerful. The poorest of the poor have an intrinsic dignity and can be great saints, outstanding models. In other places Jesus pointed out that wealth, and especially an unseemly attachment to wealth, are impediments to being like Christ.

I sometimes quote the woman parishioner who pointed out to me that possessions cannot return your love, but money and possessions can take over our lives, harden our hearts and even in some cases become consuming passions. Then people will do almost anything for money.

In another place we have Jesus' notorious teaching that it is easier for a camel to pass through the eye of a needle than it is for a rich man to enter heaven.

Poverty is defined differently in different societies and as I mentioned earlier the materially poor can be spiritually rich. It is also true that few people in Australia are poor like many are in Africa. Basic pensions mean that many who are miserable in Australia are leading disordered lives. By the standards of history most Australians are comfortable, even rich.

Most of us are not called to practise radical poverty, because we have neither the faith nor the strength to sustain us in this way of life. But we should never allow money or possessions to become our masters.

One good measure to prevent our hearts from becoming hard and selfish is to be generous regularly to good causes; to the life of the Church and for the poor and needy here in Australia and overseas, especially through Caritas and Project Compassion during Lent. The St. Vincent de Paul Society is always seeking more volunteers to help them in their charitable work. And the number in trouble usually increases in times of financial pressure. Australia is better off than most Western countries, but people can always be found who are hurting.

I might conclude with a few words on the first reading from the Old Testament Book of Ecclesiastes on the claim that all is vanity. Vanity of vanities.

This was written before the Son of God became man, when by His taking flesh, he consecrated human life and activity. It is true that wise and rich parents can have foolish children who will dissipate the inheritance, but Christian teaching emphasises that genuine human achievements are not wasted – in our families, businesses, among friends and in society. In some mysterious way they contribute not only to keeping our society good and decent, but also to constituting the new heaven and the new earth, which will be inaugurated at Christ's return.

We Christians believe not only in the immortality of the soul, but in the resurrection of the body and the worth of material creation.

"Ready for Action"
19TH SUNDAY IN ORDINARY TIME
Wisdom 18:6-9; Hebrews 11:1-2. 8-19;
Gospel: Luke 12:32-48.

The passage we have just read is a beautiful passage – beautiful, and yet once again quite disconcerting. Don't be frightened", it says, "because the Father has given you the kingdom". So far there is no problem – but Christ then continues on, almost without a breath – "So sell what you possess and give alms". He is telling us of the virtue of poverty; of not having our treasures in this life.

According to all the premises which govern modern life, "poverty" or "being poor" should be an alien concept. To many people it is; some claim that freeing people from poverty and ignorance is the Christian message today. Yet, for some strange reason, Christians who explicitly choose a simple life are admired if not imitated, especially by those who are not Christians.

There are many reasons for this; it is partly a romantic type of kickback against the absurdities of contemporary life; of rising standards of living (not enjoyed by all) and the enormous poverty in the Third World. The demand for poverty is sometimes used to canonise class prejudices, even class warfare; oddly enough, those clamouring for a more valid expression of poverty are also loudest in their attacks on celibacy – although surely someone who appreciates poverty (and the essential principle behind it) should be deeply sensitive to the value of celibacy.

Having said all that, and recognising the mixed motives behind some of these demands, what is to be our reaction to Christ's teaching? Are we to dismiss the New Testament teaching on poverty as a cultural byproduct, alien to the Gospel message and stemming from ignorance? Or should we ignore the whole undignified clamour, and keep on as we were?

The answer is clear – Christ's teaching is meant to be taken seriously.

We certainly must reject these fatuous appeals to being "poor in spirit" as an excuse for not practising poverty. If the phrase means anything, it means something more than, and not something less than, physical poverty. Christ told his followers to sell their goods.

Christ himself in his life and teaching tells us a lot. Poverty is necessary for perfection; but because some of us are too lazy or too frightened or most importantly not called to perfection, poverty is not demanded of all.

The Catholic Church does not consist only of saints, because sin is an ancient Catholic tradition, nearly as strong as mediocrity. Many of us are worse than imperfect and over the centuries the different approaches to poverty have caused difficulties and divisions, even in the best religious traditions.

The remainder of this section from the gospel complements and completes the radical call to poverty. For those striving for perfection and especially for those not so called, love, or service, is the only absolute requirement, and for this there is no substitute and no alternative.

Christ himself lived simply, having no home, etc. He also worked hard but he did have his middle class friends (e.g., Mary, Martha) to whom he could escape away from the apostles. He might have needed such an escape!

All of us have to be ready for action with our lamps lit for the master to return from the wedding, no matter at what time He returns.

The Son of Man will return at an hour we do not expect and he does not want to find us abusing the employees, or feasting excessively or getting drunk. Misbehaviour will be punished to different degrees, with the ignorant suffering less and those who should have known better receiving bigger punishments.

Much more is expected of those of us who had good parents and friends as children and received an excellent upbringing.

Here we have the parable of the talents explained in concrete fashion. Christianity is not only for champions. What is more important is how we use the gifts we have been given. Treasures in heaven do not wear out.

"Fire and Division"
20TH SUNDAY IN ORDINARY TIME
Jer 38:4-6, 8-10; Heb 12:1-14;
Gospel: Luke 12:49-53.

The three readings we have for today's Mass are not the most cheerful in the Scriptures, because all of them emphasise the cost of discipleship for every God-fearer. Christ claims he has come to bring fire to the earth and to provoke divisions not peace.

We must always remember that there is no cost-free following of Christ. We all have to keep running steadily in the race for salvation. Indeed this is always a good starting point to evaluate religious claims, because any religion which claims that it imposes no burden, makes no personal requirement on its followers is a sham. What is valuable always comes at a price and there is no human achievement without hard work and persistence.

There is something attractive in Our Lord's claim that he has come to bring fire down on the earth, and we shall return to the topic to discuss the nature of this fire. Probably the biggest danger today is from a deadly indifference and boredom.

It is more disconcerting to hear that Jesus has not come to bring peace on earth, but division. He then lists the varieties of household problems although he does not list divisions between husbands and wives.

Counter examples to this passage quickly come to mind. The usual greeting of the bishop at the start of Mass is "peace be with you". Also at Mass we exchange the sign of peace after reciting the Our Father to demonstrate that we are true followers of the Lord, and when we invoke three times the Lamb of God, who takes away the sins of the world, we twice ask for mercy and conclude by requesting that peace be granted to us.

I suppose too that all serious adult Catholics and Christians appreciate that there does come a Christian peace of heart, lying underneath whatever troubled situation in which we might find ourselves, intimately connected with a sense of purpose and direction based on the conviction that God loves us and has forgiven our sins through Jesus' redeeming activity.

Before attempting to reconcile these apparent contradictions, we must remember again that as Catholics we are followers of the Christ revealed to us in the gospels, before we adhere to a set of principles or identify ourselves in a community of his followers. In fact all three activities cannot be separated and occur simultaneously, but the logical priority is that we are followers of Jesus.

It also goes without saying that we cannot blot out from our image of Jesus those gospel passages we find unacceptable or difficult. We have to wrestle with all the gospel teaching and the solemn teachings of the Catholic Church on Jesus, especially the teaching of the early Ecumenical Councils. The temptation of every age is to reshape Jesus in its own image and once in a while in today's media, when I hear of the wimpish, all-tolerant Jesus who will approve of any sort of nonsense and many brands of evil, I wonder whether the speakers have read the gospels.

The first point to be made about the fire that Jesus brings is that it is the fire of love and it is certainly not the fire of hate and violence. Early Christianity did not expand through military conquest, but suffered 300 years of intermittent persecution. Jesus himself was a not a man of violence and told his friend Peter, in the garden of Gethsemane when he was betrayed by Judas, to put his sword away.

Secondly we have to acknowledge that the pure love of God, when injected into the human situation, provokes a moment of judgement (*krisis* is the Greek word), needs a decision between good and evil or faith and fear. This comes not from God, but from the evil in men's hearts. In the Lukan infancy narrative we hear that the child Jesus will cause "the fall and the rise of many in Israel" (Lk 2:34). A sword of sorrow pierced Mary's soul at these words and later even some in Jesus' family thought that he was out of his mind.

Jesus' own baptism (of water or fire?), which he mentions in this context, is an unusual word but refers to his later passion and death.

Early Christian history gives witness to the opposition of elements in both the Jewish and pagan populations against those who chose to follow the Lord.

Scripture scholars are sometimes reluctant to concede that the words we find in Jesus' mouth in the gospels were actually spoken by him and they indulge in interesting and sophisticated reasoning to justify their excisions. However most New Testament scholars, including many of the liberals, believe these challenging words do come from the Lord himself. He did come to bring fire.

We also find parallel sayings in the Coptic Gospel of Thomas, probably the most respectable of the many apocryphal (or false) gospels. It is even possible, although we cannot be sure, that a genuine saying of Our Lord survives here or there in the apocrypha, which is not found in the four canonical gospels. In this gospel of Thomas, we hear Our Lord claiming "He who is near me is near the fire".

I often say to our youth leaders that we need them to bring fire into the Church, to fan it into flame and we need their elders and betters to prevent them burning down that same Church!

The author of the letter to the Hebrews tells us that Our Lord, "for the sake of the joy which was still in the future ... endured the cross, disregarding (its) shamefulness". So we too should persevere in our Christian witness whatever the small, middly or large obstacles in the daily round of our duties.

Christus vincit. Christus regnat. Christus imperat.

Christ conquers. Christ reigns. Christ rules – but only through the sufferings of the Cross.

"The Good Thief"

21ST SUNDAY IN ORDINARY TIME
Is 66:18-21; Heb 12:5-7, 11-13;
Gospel: Luke 13:22-30.

"How many people will go to Heaven?" or "Will only a few be saved" are usually questions asked by people of faith, i.e., believers in the one true God, believers in life after death, and usually believers in God's judgement, in accountability to God for what we do with our lives.

Modern unbelievers are more likely to state that they do not believe in life after death for anyone; while others, preferring to ignore Christian teaching in the matter, explain that they do not know what to believe.

We are all influenced by the world around us, and we Catholics, not merely those of us who worship regularly, are only a minority here in Australia, where irreligious forces regularly batter us because we do not subscribe to their opinions. On this question of the afterlife there are quite a few Christians who have formed their views on heaven (but not on hell) from the world around us, as well as the bible. So they continue to believe in life after death and come dangerously close to asserting the right of every human being to heaven. The language of universal human rights is a wonderful development, but rights without a corresponding emphasis on responsibilities are a nightmare and rights language is used for the strangest purposes, e.g., to claim the right to an abortion, or the right to have a child by same sex couples.

There is nothing in Christian teaching to justify the claim that everyone has a right to life after death, much less to an eternity of happiness beyond human comprehension. In fact I have long suspected that those who believe everyone goes to heaven are very little distance from believing that no one goes to heaven!

While there is an almost universal longing for life after death, the dead are very silent despite the claims of those, usually fraudulent or deluded, who claim to be able to make contact with the other side. We believe in life after death because Jesus Christ, the Son of God, has told us that is the way things are, i.e., there is an eternal now, an eternity of reward and punishment judged on the presence or absence of faith, love or hate in our lives.

The Scriptural images of our union with God in heaven through Jesus Christ (which is beyond our understanding) are quite reassuring and beautiful; life, light, peace, a wedding feast, wine of the Kingdom, the Father's house, the heavenly Jerusalem, paradise.

But there are also a number of New Testament texts explaining Christ's teachings on the punishment of hell, and others like today's gospel which recounts Our Lord's un-encouraging response to the question about how many are saved.

The Jews used to barricade their houses in the evenings, lock and bolt the front gate, which was usually open during the day. Jesus explained that the gate is narrow and not everyone who wishes to enter the gate will be admitted. We have to know the head of the house and he will refuse to acknowledge the wicked, even though they claimed to have dined with him.

Jesus went further than this to his Jewish hearers saying that those in heaven will come from east and west, from north and south; an explanation which should be consoling to us in Australia. He also added that some who are now last will be first and vice versa, a teaching which brings hope to most people but is not entirely reassuring to cardinals and archbishops.

The text also explains that there will be weeping and gnashing of teeth among those excluded. Apparently not everyone will make the cut! Years ago I heard a ridiculous story of a Scottish preacher who was much attached to this teaching and frequently included it in his sermons, enunciating it very clearly. After hearing this many times, eventually a gummy toothless old grandma up the front of the church interjected "What if you don't have any teeth?" "Teeth will be provided", promised the preacher.

Where do we go from here? What is the answer to Jesus' anonymous questioner about how many will be saved? Is it sentimentality or compassion that we are a bit shocked by the thought of eternal punishment for the worst sinners? Where would an unrepentant Hitler or Stalin fit into the eternal scheme of things?

The Scriptures do not give any warrant for easy reassurances that everyone will be saved. But two basic teachings should always be remembered. The first is from today's second reading to the Hebrews. We are sons and daughters of God, and children do have rights. Secondly we must always remember that Jesus told us to call God "father" and God our Father loves us. Therefore we can be sure of love, mercy and justice. God reprimands us to help us and suffering is helpful to train us, diminish our selfishness, open us to others.

We do not know how many are saved. There is no definitive Catholic teaching that any individual is in hell. I searched the Catholic Catechism in vain to check what they had to say on the matter and it was silent, but it also explained very usefully that those who go to hell do so by their own free choice. Hell is the "state of definitive self exclusion from communion with God and the blessed" (par 1033). God is predictable, reliable, just and loving. He is not out to trick us and send us downstairs unawares. Those in hell have turned their back on God

Catholics no longer believe that only Catholics go to heaven (if we ever did). The one true God loves people of all faiths and no faith, but everyone has to be genuinely seeking the light of love and goodness.

Like you, I do not know how the good God will judge disputed cases, but no one will be damned by God by an accident of birth and no one will be damned for genuinely innocent mistakes. Genuine searchers for truth struggling towards the light in love would have good claims on the Father. Like us, their service of others will be an important criterion of judgement.

Those who refuse to consider the issue of God, especially those who reject the possibility of God because accountability to God must follow are in quite a different situation. They truly do need mercy and enlightenment, so that they will not persist in their mistaken choice.

The warm hand of God is always extended towards us. The one thing necessary for us is to reach out and grasp it.

Let me conclude once again with the story of the good thief at the crucifixion.

Jesus was crucified between two thieves. One was hostile and urged Jesus to get them out of their dire situation as he was the Messiah.

His companion rebuked him, saying that they deserved their sentence, but Jesus had done nothing wrong. Then this criminal, probably a man of violence, turned and asked, "Jesus, remember me when you come in your kingdom."

He then heard the most encouraging words in the New Testament: "Truly I say to you, today you will be with me in Paradise."

"Move Up Higher"
22ND SUNDAY IN ORDINARY TIME
Ecc 3:17-20, 28-29; Heb 12:18-19, 22-24;
Gospel: Luke 14:1, 7-14.

Today's gospel shows that Jesus regarded humility as important and the Old Testament book of Ecclesiasticus, belonging to their Wisdom literature insists that all of us, especially the powerful must behave humbly if we wish to find favour with God.

We are not to take the places of honour, but to go to the lowest place, perhaps to be invited higher.

The Christian paradox is that everyone who exalts himself will be humbled, while the man who humbles himself will be exalted.

The ancient pagan Greeks did not regard humility as a virtue, although many of their dramas show that they recognised the devastating consequences of arrogance and pride.

There is a lot of tension today between the advertised goals of our individualist, free enterprise society with its exaltation of competition (whether it be for sports prizes or a few jobs with unbelievable salaries) and the Christian virtue of humility.

At first glance there could also be some tension with the way we think and act in everyday life. Thanks be to God that the days are gone when children were taught to be seen and not heard. I suppose there were such days here, at least to some extent. But from the first born children of the first settlers, the "currency lads and lasses", who were taller than their parents, confident and outspoken, Australians were not too much under the thumb! Today good parents and teachers work consistently to build up the self-confidence of youngsters and regret it when a child cannot speak up and look after herself. Is a happy self-confident child humble? Not always, because children are naturally self-centred, and need to be encouraged through love and example to think of others. We also recognise the occasional child who is too full of himself, wants always to be the centre of attention and disregards the rights of others. Such a child does lack humility. Sadly we all know adults like this too!

On the other hand it is a sadder fact that for every youngster who is big-headed, we find four or five (or nine or ten) who are lacking in self-esteem, radically short of a proper self-confidence. This is a bigger problem.

It might come as a surprise to learn that the great North African theologian St. Augustine, who died in 430, wrote *"tota Christiana religio humilitas est"*, i.e., the whole of the Christian religion is humility; while the Italian St. Benedict, who was born fifty years after Augustine's death, and was the founder of Western monasticism (and the Benedictines who provided our first two bishops in Sydney and therefore in Australia), wrote about the twelve degrees of humility in the Rule he wrote for his followers. I think it would be true to say that this is not much quoted in today's business manuals!

Before we spell out the elements in Christian humility, we might begin with the definition given by St. Thomas Aquinas, who saw humility as a moral virtue by which we did not overreach ourselves and recognised our limitations. In other words humility is closely related to truth, to recognising the truth about ourselves and others; but it goes much further than that.

Christians generally accept that there are four cardinal virtues: justice, prudence, fortitude i.e. courage and perseverance; and temperance or moderation. Humility is one aspect of temperance, because it restrains exaggerated ambition and self-esteem while avoiding self-abasement, such as exaggerating our weakness to fish for compliments, or genuinely refusing to recognise our strengths. Genuine humility means moderation and modesty in our self-understanding. Churchill once said of a political opponent that he was a modest man with much to be modest about. Such a claim showed that Churchill was not excessively humble.

One essential mark of Christian humility is the explicit recognition of the fact that God is God, the Lawgiver, as well as Creator and loving Father. We have obligations to the one true God and we have no warrant to rewrite His rules to suit ourselves. The hallmark of Satan was that he refused to serve, and a good deal of contemporary obfuscation on conscience, even among Christians, is designed to obscure the fact that some want to be autonomous like their secular peers and rewrite whole sections of moral teachings according to modern understandings.

Humble people are also courteous, regularly striving to act with gentleness in their daily living, so that they curb their inclinations to pride, that evil growth which can take root in each one of us as the author of Ecclesiasticus explained. Habits of courtesy are particularly useful when we feel grumpy or when we feel insulted or hard done by. Courtesy is one of the best outer defences as we strive to acquire genuine humility.

Humble people are not required to sacrifice their Christian convictions; nor are they required to be doormats, to acquiesce to every contrary worldly opinion. Genuinely humble people are often strong forces for faith and goodness, not just because of the integrity of their example, but because they cannot be blown or knocked off course through ambition, flattery or abuse.

An exaggerated and false view of oneself is the direct opposite of humility. I remember an American psychologist explaining that the two groups in the U.S.A. then with the highest self-esteem were prisoners in the jail system and some of the long-term unemployed in one of the racial groups. Their view of themselves was divorced from reality.

Humble people also recognise their own sinfulness, without dwelling on it neurotically, as they also recognise the more important truth that God loves them. Because they know God loves them, humble people will also ask God's forgiveness.

Nor do humble people just look after their own, after people who can return their favours. Their active sympathy is wider than this. This is the point of Jesus' small parable today about feeding those who cannot return the kindness.

May we all continue to strive for Christian humility.

"Who Comes First?"

23RD SUNDAY IN ORDINARY TIME
Wis 9:13-18; Philemon 9-10, 12-17;
Gospel: Luke 14:25-33

Many times regular worshippers have heard me explain that we need to be clear about the basic Catholic claims, that we should not get lost in the detail, not be smothered by complexity.

I regularly tell both primary and secondary school students that they too need to be clear about these basics. They need to know that the one true God loves them, especially when they are in trouble; that Jesus Christ the only Son of God died and rose again to redeem them; that they belong to Jesus' followers, the Catholic Church, a community of worship and service led by the Pope and bishops and that they too must follow Christ, must repent and believe in the Ten Commandments.

The first reading from the Old Testament Book of wisdom asks who can know God's intentions, what the divine will might be. The author points out that our reasoning is unsure and our intentions unstable. It is hard enough to work out what should be done on earth, the author claims, without trying to discover what is in the heavens.

Human experience would give considerable backing to these claims, especially when we remember the variety of philosophers and religions throughout the world; the three great monotheist religions of Christianity, Judaism and Islam and the two other great Eastern religions of Hinduism (actually an immense variety of religious texts and doctrines as Hinduism as a title was first devised by the British Raj to distinguish most of the Indians from Moslems and Sikhs) and Buddhism, whose founder Buddha did not speak of God.

There is no doubt that human reason is limited, even among geniuses and prophets and poets. Generally Catholics acknowledge this limitation without going to the lengths of scepticism espoused by some Protestants, who believe that our intellect is so darkened by original sin that we can know very little about God by our reason; that we have to rely almost exclusively on God's special revelation in the Scriptures to know about God and even how we should live in everyday life.

Traditionally Catholics have shown more confidence in the power of reason to acknowledge the one true God and to recognise how we should live through the principles of the natural law.

Despite his scepticism the author of the Book of Wisdom is also running his argument along similar lines, because he especially recognises that God sent his Holy Spirit and Wisdom to teach us what pleases God. In his defence we must concede that we are much better placed than he was because Jesus has come among us. We are New Testament people.

However, while the basic claims of the Catholic Church are clear, they are certainly controversial, only followed at some considerable personal cost and they leave plenty of room for mystery and puzzlement.

The gospel passage today is one of the most provocative in the New Testament where we have Jesus stating that if we do not hate father, mother, brothers, sisters and our own life too, we cannot be his disciple. There is another milder version of this in Matthew's gospel (10:37) where we are required to prefer Jesus ahead of all these close relatives and our own life.

A couple of preliminary clarifications might be helpful. The commentators point out that at that time many people were following Jesus for a variety of reasons: the "great crowd" accompanying him mentioned at the start of excerpt. The experts suggest that Our Lord wanted to remind them what he was about, that he was not a travelling circus, but interested in obtaining their commitment to him and his teaching. His remarks were designed to shake their complacency and make them consider their options.

Secondly, we should also remember that Jesus often stated his principles in a startling way and then leaves us to work out the qualifications, what is possible for us and what the core demands are.

This is the significance of the two practical examples he gives; one of them quite politically incorrect when it talks of a king deciding whether he can go to war with only half the number of soldiers that his opponent has. The first example explains that there is little point in beginning to build a tower if you only have sufficient money for the foundations.

Jesus seems to be saying that the cost of discipleship is high and people should think carefully before signing on as a follower. In the days when there were many more adult baptisms, these texts would have been used as an excuse to delay baptism until late in life. People felt that they could not keep all the Christian obligations, especially as the church's penitential disciplines for sins and failures were so strict; so they waited. The first Christian Emperor in the fourth century, Constantine, was such a figure, baptised only on his deathbed.

Jesus is making three points in this passage. The first is that He himself, Jesus as the Son of God, comes first. We cannot follow him and say my family right or wrong, because family members like us stand under the Word of God. It is not right for family members to break the law or refuse to follow the commandments simply because they are family. We should be people of principle and if we are Jesus' followers we should be people of Christian principle.

Secondly if we are followers of Jesus we cannot always take the easy way. In his words we have to take up our cross. There is no cost free following of Christ, as we have to be self-disciplined and able to deny ourselves on some occasions.

The third condition is not met literally by most followers of Christ, but is the reason why members of religious orders take a vow of poverty, together with vows of chastity and obedience. They do not own anything themselves, do not take a salary, as ownership is vested in their religious orders.

Most of us do not have the capacity to live as the poorest of the poor, to own nothing as, e.g., Mother Teresa's sisters, the Missionaries of Charity, do. But we should admire those who are able to follow Christ as closely as that.

However in a crisis, Jesus would not want us to abandon Him and Christian principles simply because it would cost us money, or our position, or our possessions. This is why we venerate the Christian martyrs, those prepared to sacrifice life itself rather than deny Christ or His Church.

This passage about giving up all our possessions is a provocation and a challenge. May we have the insight to understand the teaching and the courage to put it into regular practice. And finally may we pray, as one version of the Our Father prayer makes clear, that we are not put to the test, that we are not put into crisis situations where we have to choose between God and members of our family, between God and our position or possessions.

"The Parable of the Prodigal Son"

24TH SUNDAY IN ORDINARY TIME

Gospel: Luke 15:1-32.

See 4th Sunday of Lent

"The Wisdom of the Sinner"
25TH SUNDAY IN ORDINARY TIME
Amos 8:4-7; 1 Tim 2:1-8;
Gospel: Luke 16:1-13.

Today we have Jesus' most controversial parable about the unjust steward, who was dismissed by his boss and worked to secure his uncertain future by reducing by fifty or twenty per cent the debts owed to his master. The parable does not suggest that he was entitled to do this and concludes with the master commending his former steward for his energy and his astuteness.

I have always viewed this story through good Catholic spectacles and was never tempted to believe that Jesus was commending dishonesty, even when it might not have been too clear to me what Our Lord was recommending.

Across the centuries however individuals have been scandalised and we can find more debate and discussion here than on any other parable.

We know that Constantine was the first Christian emperor, one of a long line, who granted religious freedom to Christians in 313 with the Edict of Milan. Most of the succeeding emperors were increasingly favourable to Church interests rather than religiously neutral, but as Christians were probably only one-seventh of the population at the time of Constantine, there was considerable pagan opposition to the Church for many generations, often led by the senatorial elite. Country people too were usually slower to convert than city dwellers.

One emperor who was bitterly hostile and attempted to restore paganism and destroy Christianity by every means just short of outright persecution was Julian the Apostate, the nephew of Constantine the Great, who ruled briefly from 361-363. We were fortunate that he was killed by a Persian arrow, in one of the many battles with the Romans' great Eastern rival, the Persian Empire.

Julian believed that the parable of the unjust steward praising a scoundrel was evidence of the inferiority of the Christian faith and its founder!

It is interesting to note that all of the expert commentators, ranging from the orthodox to the liberal sceptics, believe that this parable was spoken by Our Lord, although there is some dispute whether the comment about the children of this world being more astute than the children of light was spoken by Jesus in this instance or brought here from some other situation by Luke himself.

We should be clear that the parable in many ways follows the patterns we find generally in Jesus' parables. Apart from the fact that the point of many parables is somewhat unclear and puzzling (which helps explain the difficulties primary school children have in understanding them), Jesus usually avoids having unambiguously good people as the models in his stories. The Good Samaritan is the most obvious exception, although he is unacceptable and unexpected because he belongs to a despised group of foreigners; although the prodigal son, the sinful tax collector in the temple, the labourer who arrived to work at the last hour, the man who bought the field knowing a treasure was hidden there, the judge who feared neither God nor man, are all disreputable in some way or other.

Jesus used contrasts to make his point, so the dishonesty of the steward is to be emphasised not ignored. If this crook could realise his predicament and act decisively to remedy his situation, how much more important it is for good people to act energetically and seize their opportunities. The dishonest steward is not to be imitated in every way, but in one respect only.

Our Lord wanted to provoke his listeners into pondering their situations, to go below their usual surface reactions, to enter into the life of grace and there to find truth and embrace commitment.

Everyone at some stage or other finds themselves in a crisis situation, either through their own sins or bad judgement or even through factors entirely beyond their control. We need to be able to react properly to our own failures, not to sulk by wallowing in our misfortune, not to give up and abandon hope of improving but to search energetically and imaginatively for solutions. Probably the message from Luke's gospel is never to lose heart, never to give into despair about one's own failures or the failures of others.

And a final word about money, that tainted thing, which in itself is not one of heaven's riches, but can be used to come closer to God and for the work of the Kingdom. What is clear in the gospel and in everyday life is that no-one can be the slave of both God and money. We have to choose.

Personal prosperity is no guarantee that we will be generous and being short of money is no guarantee that we will avoid greed. Being short of means or short of cash can become an easy and deceitful excuse for us not to be generous.

To my initial surprise I discovered that Our Lord spoke against the dangers of riches more frequently than he spoke against hypocrisy. Long journeys start with small steps and fidelity in small matters will stand us in good stead in times of stiffer trial. This is true when we are handling money.

We should always try to be generous regularly. But if we

regularly find ourselves in a situation where we say we would like to help but cannot afford to do so at this moment, then we should examine our hearts very carefully indeed.

"Who Will be First in Heaven?"
26TH SUNDAY IN ORDINARY TIME
Amos 6:1, 4-7; 1 Tim 6:11-16;
Gospel: Luke 16:19-31.

The Old Testament prophet Amos was an outsider, a herdsman of Tekoa and a curator of sycamore trees while Jeroboam was King of Israel and Uzziah was King of Judah between 760 BC and 750 BC. Amos did not belong to any prophetic group or family line, claiming simply that God had chosen him for the role of prophet. Historically he is the earliest of the Old Testament prophets whose writing remains for us.

Decades of prosperity and peace had seen the pagan religions make progress among the Jewish people and had exacerbated the divisions between the very rich and the poor in a society where few people were in the middle and even the rich then did not live as comfortably as most Australians now do.

The first readings today and on last Sunday are taken from Amos and in both of them Amos is rebuking the rich for trampling on the needy and oppressing the poor by swindling them when paying for their products; living in luxury and not being at all interested in the mass of people living around them in misery and distress.

Usually the Catholic Church in Australia celebrates Social Justice Sunday on this Sunday. When I was a member of the Australian Catholic Bishops' Conference Social Justice Committee I suggested that they consider choosing another Sunday for Social

Justice because today coincides with the grand final weekend in a couple of football codes when many people are distracted. I confess that the problem would be greater in the four Southern states than in our own New South Wales, but, in any event the Committee did not change the date.

I suspect that one important reason for not changing would be the readings for these two Sundays which emphasise the social obligations for public life and in our personal business dealings which flow from the teachings of Scripture both in the Old Testament and from the teachings of Jesus as we see in today's parable.

Today's readings emphasise that wrongdoing and especially injustice should be punished and two of the readings set the struggle between good and evil in the context of eternity, of the afterlife. The psalm leaves us in no doubt that God is on the side of the oppressed, the hungry, and the stranger and will thwart the path of the wicked.

The four last things of Christian theology are death, judgement, heaven and hell. The awareness of death is universal especially as we become older, with an occasional ache and pain, and more importantly, as more of our friends depart for eternity. Heaven is still believed in by the vast majority of Australians, but judgement and hell have receded in the public imagination, and the depth of conviction about their existence has even weakened in the Catholic community. The four last things are still "in" because God has organised life in this way. A popular unease and scepticism about judgement and hell cannot extinguish them as realities; that is not in our power.

Today's parable, found only in Luke's gospel, forms part of chapter sixteen where it is paired with last week's parable on the unjust steward. There are two parts to this parable; a) the complete reversal of fortunes in this life and the next for the rich man and Lazarus, the poor beggar and b) the warning that those who will not listen to Moses and the prophets would not listen to any other messenger, even one who returned from the dead. Dives was dressed in purple and fine linen and feasted magnificently every day. The doctors today would explain that it is not surprising that he died young. Poor Lazarus, who was locked outside eating scraps, was covered in sores and licked by the dogs. In the next life the boots were on different feet.

From a Christian perspective, there are differing views on what it means to be poor or poor in spirit, although it is clear as a minimum requirement that we must use wealth and possessions prudently. We have obligations to others, not just to ourselves and family, and our Government reflects this in the different levels of taxation.

But there is no ambiguity at all about the requirement for Christians that we be sensitive to the suffering of those around us from poverty, sickness or any other misfortune and we must be prepared to act constructively to help. The first reading from the Old Testament prophet Amos is scathing in its condemnation of those snugly ensconced in Zion, sprawling on divans, feasting on lamb and veal and drinking wine by the bowlful, who do not care in the slightest for the fate of others, the fate of the poor and unfortunate.

The point of Jesus' parable is not so much to criticise the rich man for his sumptuous way of life, but to emphasise the criterion for the final judgement and separation between the good and evil in chapter twenty-five of St. Matthew: the rich man's heart was totally closed to the suffering of the beggar at his gates. He could not have cared less about him. We now believe that when we ignore those suffering, we ignore Christ himself. When we help the battlers, we help Christ himself.

There is a similar Egyptian folktale discovered on a document dated just after Jesus' time and others like it in later Jewish rabbinic literature. We do not know whether Our Lord knew something of these or even whether they existed in oral or written form at that time, but there is no reason to dispute Jesus' authorship. It contains an important message for all Australians who define themselves as middle class (an immense majority) and for rich Australians.

The call to faith requires a response from us. We are called to repentance and action; service and prayer as well as belief. Serving the poor and marginalised is one important part of fighting the good fight of faith and winning for ourselves the eternal life to which we are called. We should be generous regularly.

"The Duties of Servants"
27TH SUNDAY IN ORDINARY TIME
Hab 1:23, 2:2-4; 2 Tim 1:6-8, 13-14;
Gospel: Luke 17:5-10.

This is a strange, but rich gospel, which contains unrelated sayings of Our Lord on faith and duty, touching on different aspects of discipleship, set in the context of His journey to Jerusalem.

The topics of faith and duty are important and the consequences which follow from being faithful and dutiful are enormous. Today I will talk on faith.

Earlier in my priesthood the young people I was dealing with tended to equate faith with goodness, so that the accusation that a person was faithless or had little faith was seen as an accusation of personal moral evil. This was a misunderstanding as reality is more complicated. As an example, serious criminals can have genuine faith. I have often recounted the story of the Catholic jail chaplain explaining that a well known Catholic criminal regularly attended the jail Mass. When asked whether he took Communion, the chaplain explained "of course not. He has genuine faith and knows that his moral life is too disordered to go to Communion". On the other hand, all of us would know good upright people, who seem unable to believe in God, or the divinity of Christ.

Faith is not a "given", a quality we receive from nature, like the ability to be a good sprinter or distance runner; or outstanding ability at maths or music.

Certainly it is a great help to have parents of faith, where we can learn from their example and follow it. And certainly we can and should deepen our faith through regular prayer, good living and study. If a person is highly educated in some secular field but has a theological understanding typical of a thirteen year old, problems and tensions must follow.

When we pray the Lord's Prayer, taught us by Jesus himself, the translation we use has us praying "lead us not into temptation". The meaning and the more correct translation of the Greek is disputed here as some pray not to be put to the test, forced into a time of trial. Still others see the phrase as a request for help so that we will not succumb, give in when we are tempted.

Both thoughts are useful to us as Christians and some scholars claim that the two different English translations could be used for an ambiguous text. For our purposes we should remember that temptations and trials arrive not only in the realm of morals, but that our faith also can come under enormous strain through external circumstances or through our own sinful behaviour.

Faith can be tried sorely by natural disasters such as drought or earthquakes, and in those situations others have to be the hands of God and help those in trouble.

Habakkuk lived in a time of oppression and turmoil and we cannot be sure whether the threats were coming from Chaldeans or Assyrians or some other source. But in any terrible crisis, where law and order break down, participants are forced to deepen their faith or lose it at least temporarily. Where is God in that extreme suffering? Where was God in the Nazi extermination camps and the Soviet Gulag which killed even more people? It is very prudent to pray regularly that we not find ourselves in extreme situations, not be brought to times of trial in faith as well as morals.

Habakkuk tells us that God never forgets us, especially in terrible trials, even when the vision comes slowly; but come it eventually does to console us.

The spread of Christian faith across two millennia is a fascinating story, because Our Lord and the twelve apostles were certainly not well placed in a strategic sense for an assault on civilisation. In fact the progress of the Church is an example of the mulberry bush uprooting itself into the sea and then flourishing.

Today with our institutions, networks and larger numbers, we are much better placed (humanly speaking) than the apostles ever were to spread the Good News. However the problem seems to be that too often our faith is less than that of the mustard seed.

I wonder too whether we suffer from another disadvantage. Once I was discussing the principle of double effect and trying to give clear, everyday examples everyone would accept. One example: the higher number of people who are educated the more people there are with breakdowns and nervous illness.

Faith is offered first of all to the poor and dispossessed. Education usually removes us from among the poor in every sense. Is one price of education, not just a plurality of theological views, but often a significant increase of difficulty in believing; even in continuing to believe? The answer is not to reject secular education, but to complement it with appropriate religious or theological education.

When we consider the challenge of faith in the wider community, two factors make faith harder: materialism or love of money; and sexual irresponsibility, the hedonism urged upon us by many elements in the media. We learn in the beatitudes that "the pure in heart see God" and both these vices dry up our hearts, make it more difficult for the eye of the heart to see.

Let us conclude now by praying in thanks for the gift of faith, for our exemplars and mentors in the faith, parents or family or teachers and friends and let us pray that we will not be put to the test too often in matters of faith or morals.

"One Grateful Leper"
28TH SUNDAY IN ORDINARY TIME
2 Kg 5:14-17; 2 Tim 2:8-13;
Gospel: Luke 17:11-19.

It is interesting to ponder how a dispassionate and accurate observer of Catholic communities throughout the world, or the English speaking world would describe us.

There would be immense differences with the communities varying between the good and the indifferent, but what would be our better characteristics? Some such come to mind quickly: people of faith, devoted to Christ and His Blessed Mother, prayerful, working to support family life despite the wounds, deep or slight, that exist in every family, loyal to one another, genuinely helpful to the poor, whether they be close by or overseas, etc, etc.

Would we be characterised as people who were grateful for their blessings, people who knew how to say thanks to God and to one another regularly? Or would some of us be numbered among those silly people who claim that they did it all by themselves? Or would some of us belong to another group who are genuinely grateful, but are too busy or preoccupied to say so? How many of us would belong to that small number who seem constitutionally unable to express their thanks, especially to those who are closest to them?

The story of the ten lepers is not a parable, nor an incident that tells us only about the Jews of Our Lord's time. It recounts an actual incident as Jesus was travelling through Samaria and Galilee, but the story tells us a lot about human nature. It is a story about ourselves, about the way we can become if we give into selfishness regularly.

This is a good gospel passage to use with younger children, and for all sorts of reasons. With our marvellous standards of medicine, we find it hard to imagine a society with no real hospitals, few effective medicines and where if there was a surgeon of any sort it was probably a second job for the local butcher.

In those days, and indeed until the nineteenth century, there was no cure for leprosy. Because it was contagious, the social consequences of contracting the disease were extreme. Lepers were dragged from their families and isolated, forced to live in communities on the edge of society and compelled to warn people of their approach. They were outcasts, objects of fear and probably the unthinking youngsters of the district would taunt them and throw stones at them.

We think of St. Damian of Molokai (the island in Hawaii) in the 19th century, a Belgian priest who went to live with the lepers who were isolated there. Until he came the island was a like a hell; people without hope, some of them without any pretence to dignity or self-restraint. He brought hope and Christ's love to them, before himself contracting the disease.

There was no cure for leprosy in the nineteenth century; much less in Our Lord's time.

Therefore a cure for leprosy was then a spectacular miracle. Today doctors can usually control and cure it with medicines. Do we ever stop to thank God for the blessings we enjoy with our modern way of life, for the spectacular achievements of today's medicine? As Christians, I think we should!

As this was such a spectacular miracle why did nine out of ten fail to return and say thanks to Jesus? I cannot believe that they were ungrateful. For the rest of their lives, they would have remembered Jesus with gratitude.

I suspect that they were so excited with their cure, so keen to return to their families and rejoice in their good fortune that they never thought to say thanks to the miracle worker personally.

Another couple of unanswerable questions relate to Jesus' unusual request that they present themselves to the priests. I wonder whether any of them refused to go, mumbling to themselves that as Jesus could not perform the miracle, why should they bother to go to the priest!

As they were cured on their way to the priests, I wonder how many continued on to do as they were asked and actually completed their visit to the priests. It is possible that the priests did not fare much better than Jesus. The only man who thanked Jesus was a foreigner, and a Samaritan, belonging to a race the Jews did not like.

The small regular courtesy of saying thanks to those who do us small favours is good training so that we are grateful for more important blessings, such as our faith. Knowing about the Son of God is an important reason for gratitude.

If youngsters are taught to say thanks when they are young, they are more likely to remain grateful as adolescents and young adults, when they become more aware of our failings as parents, teachers, priests, grandparents. Saying thanks and meaning it requires practice. It becomes easier if we start young and keep it up. Regular thankfulness should be one characteristic of every Catholic community.

The canonisation of Mary MacKillop as Saint Mary of the Cross is a reminder that we must remember to express our gratitude not only to the "Brown Joeys" and the "Black Joeys", the two different Josephite orders; but to express our thanks to all the religious and especially the nuns who have given such high quality service, usually in quiet, unfashionable ways and places, since Catholic life began on this continent.

The different Australian colonies had difficult beginnings, some like New South Wales as convict colonies, partly because the British could not export their prisoners any longer to the newly independent United States of America. The climate was harsh and the society itself raw and often violent. An early Spanish visitor was horrified to discover there was no church building in the settlement. In fact a small Protestant chapel had been built in 1795, seven years after the first settlement, but was soon burnt down! Our St. Mary's was only opened in 1834, forty-six years after the First Fleet arrived.

Many good people worked hard to change this, but the nuns in particular were a marvellous force across the generations. Today we should pray in thanks for all their prayers and sacrifices, for the fact that nearly all the Protestant versus Catholic antagonisms have vanished as Christian combine to resist a noisy and persistent minority secularism.

"No Faith?"

29TH SUNDAY IN ORDINARY TIME
Exodus 17:8-13; 2 Tim 3:14-4:2;
Gospel: Luke 18:1-8.

The gospel today from St. Luke has Our Lord telling us of the parable of the unjust judge, who eventually gives justice to the persistent widow to get rid of her. The crooked judge is used as an image of God, a shocking and scandalous comparison. The lesson is however clear. If an unjust judge will reward perseverance, how much more will our loving God listen to us, even if He does not, perhaps cannot, intervene to answer our prayers short of a miracle.

But miracles do happen and on many occasions persistence is rewarded in unexpected ways short of the miraculous. As St. Francis of Assisi once explained: "If God feeds the unjust, we should not be surprised that He looks after his own children"!

The successful protagonist in this parable is the widow. The judge seems to have no interest in her case, probably because she had little money to pay any legal expenses at a basic or inflated cost. According to the gospels widows were listed with the orphans and strangers as the most vulnerable members of society. But in this case her persistence was rewarded.

This parable is often linked with the parable of the man wanting bread for his family at midnight from his neighbour, who is already in bed with his family. He eventually gets out of bed and gives the bread to obtain some peace. It is another unusual parable, stressing the importance of persevering in prayer and with an equally strange image of the un-altruistic head of family, who finally acts in a kindly way.

In the Our Father, Our Lord asks us to pray for our daily bread and in these parables he is reminding us to persevere in prayer especially when the praying seems pointless. He is not implying that our particular prayers will be answered, although Moses' prayer for the Jews in their struggle with the Amalakites was answered. Moses persevered with a little help from his friends. But Jesus is assuring us that God his Father loves us, is listening to us and eventually justice will prevail, all will be well, even if we have to wait until we enter Heaven.

On many occasions the progress of the Kingdom of God is impeded or sidetracked. But we are called to persevere in prayer and action.

Jesus recognises explicitly that the judge is unjust, and this probably expresses something of his views on the general way the law was enforced then. Certainly we know from the way that Herod Antipas disposed of John the Baptist that there was no rule of law as we understand it today.

Jesus promises that God will ensure that justice finally triumphs, before adding an afterthought, asking a question. "When the Son of Man comes, will he find any faith on earth?"

For me, these are the most disturbing lines in the whole of the New Testament. As the number of unbelievers grows and religious practice declines in Australia and nearly everywhere in the Western world are Our Lord's words addressed to us?

Like the persistent widow we must keep up our prayers and efforts so that the flame of faith will be passed on and that the Son of Man will always find faith in Australia.

"The Pharisee Condemned"
30TH SUNDAY IN ORDINARY TIME
Sirach 35:12-14, 16-19; 2 Tim 4:6-8, 16-18;
Gospel: Luke 18:9-14.

The parable of the Pharisee and the tax collector is one of the Lord's best known parables, ranking with the parable of the prodigal son. In my youth it was often described as the parable of the Pharisee and the publican, to the detriment of our hotelkeepers. Without doubt the title of tax collector is more accurate, although the role of the tax collector today, still somewhat unpopular, is very different from the Jewish situation two thousand years ago.

Tax collectors then had a bad public reputation. The tax collection was privatised and they retained what they collected above the quota required by the non-Jewish King Herod and the Roman overlords. It was also felt that they could be bribed and dealt unjustly with the poor. There does not seem to be any suggestion that the tax collector of the parable was a just man or even that he was a Robin Hood type of tax collector, who robbed the rich to help the poor.

Luke provides the key to the parable with his opening explanatory sentence about the listeners who prided themselves on their virtue and despised everyone else.

The commentators insists that this story would have been deeply shocking to Our Lord's hearers, especially the religiously observant, because it seems to praise a public sinner and does criticise an observant Jew who scrupulously performs his duties, avoiding adultery, greed and injustice in his business dealings. He also pays his tithes, i.e., one tenth of his income to the Jewish religious authorities.

I suspect the situation was a little more complicated than this as human nature does not warm to the proud and the religiously pretentious, although the reversal of the politically correct roles for the two main protagonists would have been provoking.

It says something about the atmosphere of faith in which I grew up and something more about the way Christ's teachings have penetrated our popular culture that I have never found the parable in any way shocking or disconcerting. In the small Catholic world of my childhood just after the Second World War none of us approved of religious show-offs, especially if we were not particularly pious ourselves (although a clear majority of my school mates worshipped each week) and we also objected to those who looked down on others for any reason at all. You might say there was more than a little of the Pharisee in us as we cheerfully and roundly condemned anyone we thought of as pharisaical! Ours was a society which prized honesty and was wary of dissemblers.

What exactly was Christ's message when he told this parable?

As a preliminary clarification we can rule out the suggestion that God was somehow unjust to the Pharisee or disliked him for no good reason. We similarly reject the suggestion that God was praising or approving the wrong doing of the tax collector.

The tax collector was humbling himself by honestly conceding that he was a sinner and asking God for mercy. He is not despairing because he asks for God's mercy, probably quoting the opening words of Psalm 51, which goes on to proclaim that God will not despise "a broken and a contrite heart".

On the other hand the Pharisee is exaggerating his goodness, concentrating solely on his good behaviour, studiously ignoring his own faults and concentrating on the faults and weaknesses of others. He condemns the general mass of people and the tax collector, whose heart is unknown to him. Here we should remember Our Lord's other statements about the blind Pharisee, who neglects the more important matters of the law, justice, mercy and faith and about the hypocrite who sees the splinter in another's eye and cannot see the plank of wood in his own!

The Pharisee is proud, loves himself, does not have much need for God, and has no manifest sympathy or love for his fellow human beings.

The parable chimes in nicely with St. Paul's teaching about the insufficiency of simply observing the precepts of the Law, of doing this in a heartless, loveless way. His religious practice is onesided and complacent.

The example of the Pharisee is not a warning for other people but a warning for each one of us. Deep in the heart of each one of us there can be a dose of the Pharisee, which chooses our ground carefully so that we can exalt our own performance or endowments or situation and look down on others.

We are always called to be honest, to be sympathetic and loving and to realise that we need God's love and forgiveness. Accurate self-knowledge is a help to faith and goodness.

"The Rich Convert"
31ST SUNDAY IN ORDINARY TIME
Wisdom 11:22-12:2; 2 Thess 1:11-2:2;
Gospel: Luke 19:1-10.

In the Jubilee Year 2000 I was privileged to accompany 200 young adults from the Melbourne archdiocese on pilgrimage through the Holy Land to the World Youth Day celebrations in Rome. It was a wonderful time both in a human and spiritual sense.

We had carefully selected and faithful youth leaders and good priests, who prepared their sermons well for the sacred places through which we passed. I have never known, before or since, anything to equal the waves of conversions which rippled through these young believers.

So many turned more intently towards God and his Son, but this was done without fanfare, fuss or fury. Many went to confession a number of times, peeling away successive layers of selfishness and sin. One young man, a fine athlete, said to one of the bishops. "Today was the best day of my pilgrimage?" "Why?" replied the bishop, "were you at Gethsemane or the tomb of the resurrection?" "No" came the answer, "I went to confession".

When we were approaching Jericho the guide stopped us near a sycamore and told us that this was the tree Zacchaeus climbed in order to see Jesus. It looked very old, but most of us were sceptical that it was the original sycamore, often called the "foolish fig tree".

Luke rarely or never described the height of any of his gospel characters. He probably did so here to explain why Zacchaeus could not easily see Jesus, although early commentators suggested this detail implied a weak faith.

Zacchaeus is a good model for us today, not because he was rich, but because he was no respecter of persons, not constrained by the opinions of others, not frightened to appear ridiculous in his determination to see the Lord.

The term Luke used for "seeking" was the same word that is used of Our Lord as he seeks out sinners. Zacchaeus, the social outcast among the Jews because he was a tax collector and belonging to the rich who could only enter heaven as a camel would move through the eye of a needle, wanted to see this prophet, this religious teacher and wonder-worker and he moved resolutely to achieve his aim. He was looking for more, probably for salvation and was rewarded.

Jesus ordered him to come down immediately because he wanted to stay at his house.

This was a huge surprise to the crowd and all of them, not just the Pharisees and scribes, complained at Jesus' visiting the house of such a sinner.

Zacchaeus was well able and used to defending himself, insisting that he gave half his goods to the poor and repaid fourfold anyone he had wronged. This latter amount reflected the penalties prescribed for stealing in the book of Exodus (c21) and the penalty for thieves in Roman law. He was stating that he was already an honest man, perhaps a disciple of John the Baptist who had laid down that tax collectors should not gather more than their due.

This is not a story of moral conversion, although some have interpreted it in this way. I remember hearing of a play where Mrs. Zacchaeus gave her husband a terrible time afterwards for giving away so much of the family's money. Once a very rich man with a strong wife came after I had recounted this embellishment in my sermon to say that he thought it true to life!

Neither did Jesus back away from his provocative invitation in the face of the crowd's objections, emphasising that salvation had come to this house and that Zacchaeus is a true son of Abraham, not because he was a Jew, but because of his faith and righteousness. The simple minded determination and enthusiasm of this rich outcast had been rewarded in a totally unexpected fashion.

Just as the blind man in Jericho had persisted in crying out for Our Lord's attention, despite the protestations of the scolders, and been rewarded with his sight, so Zacchaeus was rewarded with faith and insight.

Australians often like to think of themselves as standing on their own two feet, not capitulating too easily in front of hostile public opinion. I am not sure this self-understanding is warranted today, when we are tempted so strongly to be apologetic, self-conscious about our Catholic identity.

It would be useful if we could clone Zacchaeus again and again as a model for us today. We need brave Christians.

Nobody is born a hero, even if some are more persistent or pig-headed than others, but practice makes perfect. I remember hearing a Catholic speaker claim that a young person who successfully resisted hostile peer pressure three times on important issues made himself free for the rest of his life. This is probably true, or at least very likely.

The story of Zacchaeus is also encouraging for all comfortable middle-class or rich Australians, because it follows Jesus' warning about riches and the story of the rich aristocrat, a good young man, who was unable to follow Jesus because he was too attached to his wealth. Salvation came to Zacchaeus, but he was already following God and not money. We too have to choose, every one of us.

I still remember as a young man being exhorted by my teachers to stand on my own two feet, not to follow the crowd.

This was good advice and Zacchaeus is a model for us all.

"God of the Living"

32ND SUNDAY IN ORDINARY TIME
2 Macc 7:1-2, 9-14; 2 Thess 2:16-3:5;
Gospel: Luke 20:27-38.

Even within the Catholic Church in Australia today there is considerable confusion and ignorance on religious questions. Outside the Church I suspect the confusion is greater, which in turn also impinges on us as a minority. The long term danger is that we are taken over by the majority culture, where the most active creative elements are often anti-religious.

While readily acknowledging this general confusion, I was still shocked and surprised by a number of items in the 2007 Generation Y report, especially by the data on belief in reincarnation, i.e., that people had lived previous lives. Almost four times as many young Catholics (35%) as Anglicans (9%) believed in reincarnation and the Catholic figure was double the rate for other Christians (17%). It is not reassuring to be told that young Catholics are so much more superstitious than other young Christians!

The figures for belief in reincarnation are worse for Catholic baby boomers, i.e., those born after the Second World War (under 60s), with 41% of them believing this nonsense, while the 30-40 year old group have twice as many undecided as the Generation Y's and only three-fifths as many firmly opposed!! It is probable that a percentage of Catholics confused reincarnation with resurrection!

Years ago I never dreamed that I would have to start a sermon on life after death by insisting that Christians do not and should not believe in reincarnation, which is not taught by Christ or the Church.

Now let us return to this joust between Our Lord and the Sadducees. I probably do not need to remind you that while Jesus sometimes taught in synagogues, especially at Capernaum, he generally spoke to mixed crowds in the open. His followers were there, probably a larger group of sympathisers, his opponents and a great mass of the idle, unemployed, the curious and always a number of sick and disturbed people hoping for a cure. They wanted to hear what Jesus would say and how he would deal with the interjectors and opponents.

A second piece of background is to give a little information on the Sadducees. Just as Christians today are divided into Catholics, Orthodox, Anglicans and Protestants so there were first of all the Pharisees, strict, sometimes fanatical. Jesus' strongest critics and most of his followers came from among them. There were also small communities of Essenes, not mentioned in the New Testament.

When the Jews returned from the Babylonian captivity the descendants of Zadok the High Priest were given the privilege of providing the priests for the Jerusalem Temple. Zadok is remembered in the beautiful anthem composed by Handel which is always sung at the coronation ceremonies in Westminster Abbey for the Kings and Queens of England.

The Sadducees were connected with this group, but had expanded beyond the priests to become a small powerful circle of Hellenised aristocrats – the Jewish ruling establishment, with very little popular support. This is the only occasion on which they are mentioned in Luke's gospel, although they appear more frequently in Matthew.

Thoroughly liberalised and tempted to scepticism rather than fanaticism, they did not believe in the resurrection of the body. Probably many of them did not believe in the immortality of the soul either, or in any form of personal life after death.

It is interesting to note that the objector phrased his question in a story, a type of parable. One commentator suggests it was a typical Sadducee objection to the Pharisees' position, who did believe in the resurrection of the body, but I am not so sure. The crowd would have appreciated a new angle and an old objection would have left Our Lord too well placed to answer.

Against the Sadducees Jesus clearly emphasised his belief in life after death (and we basically believe in life after death because of his teaching), but he explained that life in heaven will be different as it will not be an earthly paradise. Marriage is an institution for this life, designed to ensure the continuity of the human race and will not be necessary in heaven.

Therefore the problem for the wife whose seven husbands, all brothers, who predeceased her, does not arise. One wonders whether at least the younger brothers were nervous at marrying such a formidable woman! The custom of such marriages whereby a brother had intercourse with his brother's widow to continue the line was common among the Assyrians, Hittites and Canaanites and was taken into the Mosaic Law. The Sadducees were wrong to presume that such earthly institutions would continue in heaven.

It was the Greeks who believed in the immortality of the soul, while the Jews in the 500 years before Christ were more likely to emphasise the resurrection of the body. Early on the Jews only had a vague almost non-existent belief in a personal life after death. Sheol and Hades were shadowy underworlds, where God could not be praised, although by the time of the book of Daniel the resurrection of the dead was affirmed. There was no reference to the resurrection in the Torah, the original five books of Mosaic legislation. It is also of some interest that the Pharisees believed that everyone's soul continued to exist after death, but that only the good participated in the resurrection of the body. This is not Christian teaching.

In conclusion what therefore is the classical Christian teaching of the Catholic Church on life after death?

We believe in life after death, the immortality of the soul and the resurrection of the body into a changed new heaven and new earth.

We do not believe everyone has a right to the happiness of heaven, but believe in God's judgement, the separation of the sheep from the goats, of the good from the evil and selfish.

We also believe in purgatory, a time of waiting and purification so we will be worthy to enter God's presence, able to cope with His Goodness and Love. Therefore we pray for the souls of the faithful departed to speed them on their way.

In summary we believe in the four last things: death and judgement, heaven and hell.

"Terrible Times"

33RD SUNDAY IN ORDINARY TIME
Malachi 3:19-20; 2 Thess 3:7-12;
Gospel: Luke 21:5-19.

The temple in Jerusalem reconstructed by Herod the Great was an impressive building which Jesus loved and had visited since he was a child. The Jewish people revered the Temple even more than we reverence St. Peter's Basilica in Rome because only in the Temple were the sacrifices performed. Within this Temple was the Holy of Holies, the most sacred precinct which contained no sacred or precious objects in Our Lord's time, indicating dramatically the transcendence of the One True God, God's utter simplicity and spirituality.

The other synoptic gospels also report Jesus' shocking prediction that the Temple would be destroyed so that not a stone remained upon a stone. This was quite rightly seen as a judgement on the people of the Temple, just as Micah and Jeremiah had predicted the earlier destruction of the Temple by the Babylonians and described it as a judgement.

Not surprisingly Jesus' listeners asked when this was to happen and what would be the signs of the approaching catastrophe. He replied by giving some general warnings, which are listed in today's gospel before going on to describe the armies encircling Jerusalem and urging them to flee into the mountains.

As reported in Luke, Jesus' warnings are frightening enough, but they are described in terms of recognisable historical circumstances with not as much apocalyptic technicolour as the other evangelists used about the disasters which will precede the last times.

Jesus first warned about religious imposters who would claim to speak in his name. The claims of these false Messiahs are not to be believed. He then went on to speak of terrible wars and revolutions, of nation fighting against nation, but even these upheavals, he said, are not a sign that the end of the world is near.

All of Luke's readers after 70 A.D., when the Romans led by Titus (the son and successor of Vespasian as emperor) completely destroyed Jerusalem, would have read these predictions in the light of that disaster.

Even by the terrible twentieth century levels of killing in the First and Second World Wars the losses in this Jewish Roman war were remarkable.

Josephus, the Jewish writer who finished up as an historian for the Romans, tells us that 1,100,000 were slaughtered including 6,000 refugees who had gathered in the portico of the Temple, deluded by a false prophet into believing they would receive a final revelation there. 97,000 captured Jews were paraded as slaves through the streets of Rome in the triumphal procession to celebrate this victory. On the Arch of Titus which still stands near the Roman Colosseum the booty captured from the Temple is depicted, including the seven branched candlestick or "menorah".

One astute commentator has observed that Jesus' prediction of this destruction was not necessarily a purely supernatural insight. Those who understood Roman power and arrogance and the intransigence and imprudent revolutionary aspirations of the Jews would have understood they were on a collision course.

The final general sign outlined by the Lord was the persecutions, which would be launched by synagogues and the civil authorities. Even family members and friends would betray them. Some would be put to death; they would be objects of universal hatred, but in God's eyes and in the light of eternity "not a hair of (their) head will be lost" and (their) "endurance will win them (their) lives".

These predictions came to pass almost as soon as the post-resurrection preaching began. Peter was flogged in Jerusalem (Acts 5:40) and Paul was lashed five times, beaten with rods three times (2 Cor 11:24) and suffered many other calamities before his martyrdom.

Even before the destruction of Jerusalem, Nero, one of the most disgraceful, cruel and foolish of the Roman emperors, had launched his persecution after the great fire in Rome in 64 A.D.

The Roman writer Tacitus described how some of those arrested in this Neronian persecution betrayed their fellow Christians and then exemplified the widespread hostility to the "notoriously depraved Christians" whose community he regarded as "a deadly superstition" (Annals XV, XLIV).

All the small Christian communities would have been aware of that terrible period from the fire in Rome to the final capture of Masada fortress in Palestine in 73 A.D. They would have seen them as examples of the four deadly acts of judgement from the Lord, listed by Ezekiel; sword, famine, wild beasts and pestilence.

Today nearly all Christians are loathe to connect sin and suffering too closely, because Our Lord acknowledged the suffering of the innocent and the random nature of disasters.

But the wages of sins are sometimes, perhaps often, paid in this life, as well as in eternity by individuals, societies and nations.

The unjust do not always continue to prosper in this life, because pride comes before a fall and those who live by the sword regularly die by the sword.

When we are tempted to think that our lot in life is difficult – or even when it is – we can take heart in the Lord's promise that he will be with us through it all and see us through to the fullness of life with him in eternity.

"The King of the Jews"
34TH SUNDAY – FEAST OF CHRIST THE KING
Sam. 5:1-3; Col 1:12-20; Gospel: Luke 23:35-43.

Hail Redeemer, King Divine!
Priest and Lamb, the throne is Thine
King whose reign shall never cease,
Prince of everlasting peace.
Angels, saints and nations sing
"Praised be Jesus Christ, our King;
Lord of life, earth, sky and sea,
King of love on Calvary.

We celebrate once again the feast of Christ the King; Jesus Christ the Son of Mary, who lived and died to free us from our sins and rose triumphantly from the dead to vindicate finally his Divinity, his divine sonship.

We give Jesus many titles to acknowledge that he is our Lord and our God; we call Him the Messiah, the Christ, the one anointed with the oil of chrism; we call him Son of Man, Redeemer and Saviour; we do not mock him like those at the foot of the cross when we praise him as King of the Jews; Alpha we call him and Omega, the first and last letters of the Greek alphabet, to signify that Christ is the key to the immensity of the universe and to all the grandeur, folly and simple foolishness of human history. We dare to say that we are sisters and brothers of Jesus, because the one great God is our Father; this Father is Jesus' God and our God and we call Jesus King, because He is our model and teacher and leader. We are members of his Kingdom, whose values are not those of earthly Kingdoms; but it is nonetheless a Kingdom which is rooted in our hearts and in the mud and dust of human history, and which extends far back into the past, far into the future and will be consummated only in eternity.

We are disciples, followers of Christ, who rejoice in the name Christian, just as we rejoice in the title Catholic, the Greek word for universal, signifying our membership in the one world-wide family, united under the leadership of the Pope and bishops, which also goes back in an unbroken line to the time and person of Christ and his immediate chosen leaders the Apostles.

The kingship of Jesus is out of this world, provocative and unusual and even by these standards the excerpt from Luke's gospel is even more peculiar.

We do not hear today of the return of the Son of Man at the end of time to judge the living and the dead and to separate the self-centred from those who recognise Christ in the unfortunate.

Neither do we have the dignified interaction between the increasingly interested Roman governor and this condemned prisoner from the North, powerless and about to die who tells Pontius Pilate that his kingdom is not of this world, but that "Yes, I am a king", who came into the world to bear witness to the truth.

In our passage "the image of the unseen God and the first born of all creation" is on a cross about to die between two thieves and surrounded by a small hostile and jeering mob.

Even one of the two criminals is hostile, but the good thief acknowledged his guilt and the innocence of Jesus. Then he asked "remember me when you come into your kingdom". He did better than he expected: "today you will be with me in paradise".

Only a king with extraordinary powers beyond the here and now could promise this.

In the European world to which we Australians belong culturally, we have now again, for the first time in more than a thousand years, a widespread popular atheism and indifferent agnosticism, among at least 15% of our people; a neo-paganism which is still growing steadily here in Australia. In 2012, 22% of Australians declared in the census that they did not belong to any religious group. Sociologists estimate that more than half of these would believe in God, variously defined.

Some of our greatest blessings are beliefs which we Christians almost take for granted. I learnt about right and wrong from my mother's knee; learnt that my faith was a precious possession, that I should pray regularly, that there was a heaven of everlasting joy where those who suffered more than their share in this life would have it made up to them; a heaven of mercy and justice.

Many good Australians are ignorant or confused on these points, because they know little of Christ or his teaching. Somehow we must spread the light of Christ out towards them.

On this feast of Christ the King I want to mention three fundamentals or basics about our belief in Christ. I make no apology for this, because the Catholic Church has always been committed to fundamentals. We are committed irrevocably to the creeds, the sacraments and the commandments. We are committed irrevocably to the truth about Jesus, true God and true man, but the Church has never been fundamentalist, because the Church reverences the power of reason, has a magnificent theological tradition, is not a religion of the Book (although we stand under the Word of God) and believes in a living teaching authority, located ultimately in the Pope and bishops.

Firstly on this feast of Christ the King we must thank God that the Word was made flesh and dwelt among us. The one great God is immensely different, invisible, silent as death, approached certainly through the beauty and order of the world of nature and human invention, but also concealed from us by human suffering and by natural disasters.

Christ changed this through his life and teaching, because the poor and the suffering, and many of the sinners too, have been able to understand a God dying on the cross as a young man to redeem and save us. Somehow this tells them that their suffering can ultimately be turned to good, that they too can enter paradise like the good thief.

Christ makes God accessible to us. It is easier to love a fellow human than an invisible Spirit, especially when we have a human who tells us of God in the parable of the prodigal son (or loving father), who healed and helped so many, who wept over the fate of Jerusalem, who coped so kindly, but firmly, with human weakness, who was so upset by hypocrisy, and so remorselessly opposed to the idolisation of wealth, opposed to Mammon, to the restless spirit of greed and avarice, which dominates our societies and has provoked the economic crisis, the unsustainable debts made evident from 2008 onwards.

On the feast of Christ the King, we must thank God that the Word was made flesh.

Secondly we should remember, in faith and in a spirit of humble reverence and adoration, that the Jesus of Nazareth (isn't that the carpenter's son?), who was born in a stable at Bethlehem, who was run out of his home village after preaching there, who was crucified with two thieves on a rubbish tip, was and is and always will be the Son of God, the equal of the Father, the Second Person of the Triune God.

The man we follow, whose teachings we try to put into practice, however imperfectly, is not another holy man, not just a great prophet, not a philosopher, not just a mystic, but a single person with a divine as well as a human nature. Because of this He was able to redeem us, to conquer the remorseless power of evil, through his death on the cross and not despite it. Because of this his teachings have a unique status. It is for this reason that his teachings are not negotiable.

It is this Jesus, the Christ, whom Daniel foretold as coming on the clouds of heaven, who developed and changed the concept of kingship inherited from King David. His is an eternal sovereignty, a glory and kingship which will be recognised by peoples of all races and languages.

St. Paul called Our Lord the image of the unseen God, the first born of all creation and the Creator of all things on earth and in heaven.

We know that Christ the King is divine, and therefore able to forgive us our sins. Pagans cannot understand God's forgiveness.

Thirdly we should remember with deep gratitude that Christ the King showed us how much he wanted to be part of us by allowing us to take His Body into ourselves.

We eat Jesus' flesh and drink his blood. We can adore Jesus really and truly present in the bread, in the host.

The first followers of Jesus were disturbed by this and many ceased to follow him because of it. Many Christians today, and too many Catholics, are also embarrassed by this teaching, tempted to explain away the Real Presence, or are at least content not to make too much of it.

The celebration of the Eucharist in the sacrifice of the Mass is the source and summit of Christian life, and the adoration of the Blessed Sacrament is a beautiful devotion, which comes from the Mass and leads to the Mass, and is a particularly appropriate devotion for us.

I believe the greatest challenge to religion in Australia today is the challenge to faith. There are many other pressure points too, materialism, greed, disordered sexuality, but the fiercest challenge is to faith because the other disorders make it more difficult to believe.

For that reason the explicit prayer of adoration before the Blessed Sacrament is another fundamental, which is recommended by our Holy Father the Pope, which we should not forget or ignore. It is a devotion which is loved by many young Catholics, who appreciate the silence and begin to be aware of God's transcendence.

In conclusion then, may this feast of Christ the King remind us to be grateful for the gift of faith, for our understanding of these basic beliefs and practices which faith brings us. As we continue our pilgrimage may the King most holy rule our minds, our hearts, our wills and may the King of Truth bring all of us finally to eternal light.

"Body and Soul"

THE ASSUMPTION OF OUR LADY
Apoc 11:19, 12:1-6, 10; 1 Cor 15:20-26;
Gospel: Luke 1:39-56.

It is most appropriate when we celebrate our annual Mass for pregnant women on the feast of the Assumption of Our Lady.

We know that Mary has a unique spot in Catholic life, receiving honour and devotion second only to that given to her Son, Jesus Christ. When I was young the Church was criticised for paying too much attention to Our Lady and such criticism is still heard from some hard line Protestants today, despite Mary's prominence in the New Testament. More frequently, however, the Church is accused of being anti-women, because of the Catholic refusal to ordain women priests.

I do not want to set too many hares running so I should return to the feast of the Assumption, which was only decreed as an official dogma of the Catholic Church in 1950.

In the Christian East, now largely the world of the Orthodox, the feast was known as the feast of Our Lady's Dormition, or falling asleep, and we have evidence of this celebration from the fifth century.

The Catholic teaching on the Assumption is that, because of her preeminent faith and goodness which was recognised in her being chosen as the mother of God's Son, Mary was taken up body and soul into heaven at the moment of her death.

Many of the ancient pagan Greeks believed in the survival of the soul after death (immortality), but we also believe in the resurrection of the body on the last day as Christ promised. In some way we shall be body and soul in heaven. I suppose we shall be at our spiritual, moral and physical peaks, which probably will require characteristics from different periods of our lives. Most of us are not spectacularly wise or unselfish when we are young!

The first strange reading from the Book of the Apocalypse recognises Mary's immense dignity by describing her as the woman adorned with the sun, standing on the moon, with twelve stars on her head as a crown.

Her pregnancy with the Christ child is also acknowledged explicitly as she was crying aloud in the pangs of childbirth and we then have a horrible symbolic description of the struggle between good and evil, between herself and her child on the one hand and the red dragon, symbol of evil, with seven crowned heads and ten horns on the other.

But while the struggle is described for us too brutally, it is followed by an explicit claim for the victory of goodness. "Victory and power and empire for ever have been won by our God", through the life and activity of the grown Christ Child, who has gained full authority over all creation.

Mary's cooperation in all this, which is a poetic description of our redemption, is absolutely essential and indispensable. And just as Mary had a central role in the story of our redemption, so every mother has a crucial role in the total development, physical, spiritual, moral and educational of her children. This is an immense honour, but it is also a considerable responsibility. As Elizabeth exclaimed in today's gospel Mary was blessed and the fruit of her womb was blessed and in a different way a similar point must be made about every mother and child.

In the nine months of pregnancy and the long years until the child becomes an adult, the mother nurtures her child physically, emotionally and spiritually. This is a wonderful and difficult task and vocation, where the woman is called to give her all, preferably supported by a loving and energetic husband. As Pope Benedict has insisted "every child who is born brings us God's smile", although I suppose this is not as evident when they won't stop crying!

The ancient conviction that each person is unique, which is regularly confirmed as parents marvel at how different the personalities of their children are one from another, has been reinforced by modern scientific discoveries of D.N.A., the constituents of the human genome, where much of our unique development is programmed from the moment of conception.

Our talents and capacities are mightily influenced also by nurture, by the love, care and stimulus we receive in the early years from those who love us; first of all from mother and father, but especially also from brothers and sisters, grandparents, aunts and uncles. Babies are not there to be hidden away from the extended family!

Every child has a unique spiritual potential to be developed through baptism, the reception of the other sacraments and being taught to pray and believe as well as to follow the commandments of love. Parental example is crucial here.

And every new-born has the capacity to share the vision of the one true God in heaven. The baptism ceremony explains the pride and joy of every mother as she sees the hope of eternal life shining in the eyes of her child.

All these are great blessings, and on many occasions they do not come easily and without sacrifice and difficulty. I pray that no mother here today will suffer the hurt and turmoil of Mary's life: the scandal of the divine conception, Joseph's first instinct for a quiet divorce, her giving birth away from home in a stable, her flight as a refugee to Egypt and then being forced to watch the struggles and suffering of her Son's public life.

Following Christ does not guarantee us an easy life, but it does bring peace and does give us strength for difficult times.

We thank God for the fact that Australia has become friendlier to children, despite considerable unease, not all of it justified, about our immigration rate. In 2009 Australia welcomed a record number of new babies, 301,000 in fact.

Half of these births were to first-time mothers, while another third were having their second child. Another good sign was that the number of births per woman under 30 years of age increased for the first time since 1971. In 2010 the Australian fertility rate was 1.97, still not enough to maintain replacement levels, but improving. We thank God that these trends have moved slowly in the right direction and call on all political parties to help those women who want to have children and are constrained by financial pressures.

Parents who have hope, who believe in service and sacrifice for good causes, who do not believe that a high standard of comfort is the most important achievement, will have children. There is no Catholic regulation that you should only have two children, just as there is no Catholic regulation that parents must have the maximum number physically possible. But we all should remember that siblings are a blessing for one another as well as for their parents.

The feast of the Assumption teaches us many lessons. Mary's

going to heaven body and soul at her death is a vindication of the goodness of material creation, of our bodies. It reminds us of the central role of women in society, in the life cycle and in the importance of being good wives and mothers.

And the feast of the Assumption reminds us of the importance of spiritual values, of the reality of life after death and finally it reminds us of the wonderful eternal future of happiness which is the proper destiny of every baby who has been born or is yet to be born.

www.ingramcontent.com/pod-product-compliance
Lightning Source LLC
Chambersburg PA
CBHW021856230426
43671CB00006B/409